THE APOCALYPTIC TIMELINE
IN THE BOOK OF REVELATION

VOLUME 1: SEALS

THE APOCALYPTIC TIMELINE
IN THE BOOK OF REVELATION

VOLUME 1: SEALS

ANDRONICUS JOHNSON, CALEB LEE, AND AZARIA STEPHEN

http://www.apocalyptictimeline.com

THE APOCALYPTIC TIMELINE
IN THE BOOK OF REVELATION

World Ahead Press is a division of WND Books. The views and opinions expressed in this book are those of the authors and do not necessarily reflect the official policy or position or WND Books.

Paperback ISBN: 978-1-944212-48-3
eBook ISBN: 978-1-944212-49-0

Printed in the United States of America
16 17 18 19 20 21 LSI 9 8 7 6 5 4 3 2 1

All Scripture quotations are taken from The Holy Bible, King James Version (KJV) unless otherwise specified.

All Greek Scripture quotations are taken from The Holy Bible, Textus Receptus (TR) unless otherwise specified.

All Qur'an quotations are taken from The Qur'an, Sahih International, The Quranic Arabic Corpus, http://corpus.quran.com, unless otherwise specified.

The book examines how the Seals in Revelation match with the historical events, presents detailed proofs, and scrutinizes which era we live in at present time.

www.ApocalypticTimeline.com

CONTENTS

Preface   9

1. **Sequence of Events in Revelation**   **15**
    Sequential Order of Events   15
    Disclaimer   25
    Occurrence Pattern of the Prophetic Events   26
2. **The Fourth Seal: Kill with Death and Beasts**   **30**
    The Most Easily Identifiable Seal   30
    With Death, and with the Beasts of the Earth   33
    The Black Death in Europe   37
    Plagues in China and India   40
    Population Reduction in the Affected Land   44
3. **The Fourth Seal: Kill with Hunger**   **46**
    The Great European Famine   46
    Famines in China and India   51
4. **The Fourth Seal: Kill with Sword**   **55**
    The Mongol Empire   55
    Massacre by the Mongols   58
    Power Given over the Fourth Part of the Earth   59
    The Relationship among Sword, Famine,
    and Pestilence   65
5. **The First Seal: A Bow and a Crown**   **70**
    Is the Rider on a White Horse Jesus Christ?   70
    Constantine the Great   79

Theodosius the Great 82
Pope Leo I 84
How the Bishop of Rome Rose to Power 85
Clovis I 87
Justinian the Great 91
The Justinian Code 91
Interpretation of the First Seal 95

6. **The Third Seal: A Yoke** **102**
Is the Third Seal Famine? 102
Is the Third Seal Slavery? 112
The Feudal System 118
Feudalism in England 122
Life of the Serfs 124
Food for the Serfs 125
Decline of Feudalism 127
Capitalism and Labor Exploitation 127

7. **The Second Seal: Peace Taken from the Earth** **129**
Is the Second Seal a War? 129
Rise of Islam 138
Jihad and Terrorism 140
Doctrine of Jihad 145

8. **The Fifth Seal: Slain for the Word of God** **151**
Who are the Souls under the Altar? 151
The European Wars of Religion 155

9. **The Sixth Seal: Great Earthquake** **163**
The Great Lisbon Earthquake 163
Debate over the Cause 168

10. **The Sixth Seal: Sun Became Black, and
Moon as Blood** **172**
The Sun Became Black as Sackcloth of Hair 172
The Moon Became as Blood 187

11. The Sixth Seal: Stars of Heaven Fell   **189**
    The Leonids   189
    The Heaven Departed as a Scroll   195
12. The Sixth Seal: Every Mountain and
    Island Moved   **204**
    The Sumatra Earthquake   204
    For the Great Day of His Wrath is Come;
    and Who Shall Be Able to Stand?   212
13. The Seventh Seal: A Golden Censer with Fire   **217**
    The Tunguska Blast   217
    Sovereign God in Control   229

Endnotes   *230*

PREFACE

In March of 2010, we were living up to our day-to-day demanding schedule. As believers in Christ, we knew in our minds we should live every day being obedient to our Lord's will, but it was not always easy to live such a life as we hoped to. Like most people, we ironically failed to realize that we were actually living in disobedience to Christ. We even thought we were faring well as Christ's servants in our own understanding.

One day, we came across "H.R. 3200: America's Affordable Health Choices Act of 2009," the so-called Obamacare bill that stirred up the world then. We were not very interested in world news, as we had thought it was good to live dissociated from the world as Christians, so it was by chance we learned about the news.

Because many Christians believed the bill was related to the 666 mark in the book of Revelation, we decided we should also examine the issue. For the first time in our lives, we browsed through internet in search of the bill, and ended up perusing relevant sections of the bill that we downloaded from the Library of Congress. From reading, we learned about class II device that was implantable in human body.

Of course, the bill then did not stipulate that all people shall receive a mark related to the Antichrist. The bill wrote that "the Secretary shall establish a national medical device registry on the device that is a class II device that is implantable."[1] If the "class II device" here was implantable in the human body, it was possible that this bill was a bill preceding and preparing for a perhaps imminent 666 mark of the Antichrist.

Fortunately, this bill was abolished, as it did not pass the House of Representatives. But as a result, we as Christians were in great shock in light of the following facts. The technology for devices implantable in the human body had been completed and ready for use for a long time already; then, Verichip was such a device that was available in market as a possible 666 mark of the beast.

Moreover, there were people preparing to implant such devices into all human beings. Of course, their first approach would be to use the device for medical uses, particularly for diabetic patients. For example, if a chip inserted into a patient would check the blood-sugar level on a regular basis and send the data to a doctor's office, how much convenience would it bring to the medical world? But wouldn't it be terrifying if such protocol was used for personal identification purposes in effect of a legislation that mandates all people get implanted with such a device?

If such a chip is already technologically ready for use, the only possible stumbling block to inserting such a device in a body would be social resistance to such legislation that mandates implantation of a device into human body. Now let us ask: In this digital era, will the young generation reject the chip, forgoing the convenience of using it? If our expectation that the young or next generation would readily accept the chip implantation turns out to be true, would such fact imply the imminence of the return of our Lord?

Such questions as mentioned above woke us from our sleep. We turned away from our belief that we were faring well as faithful Christians, living according to the will of our Lord.

Instead, we wondered why we have been living so ignorant of world affairs when we are getting closer day by day to the second coming of our Lord.

And of course, we started studying the Bible with a new perspective, particularly the book of Revelation. In fact, we had been Christians who read the Bible on a regular basis, but we had not paid much attention to the last book in the Bible. This was because every time we read Revelation, its content was so difficult that it seemed impossible to understand.

However, with a possibility of our Lord coming soon, we needed to know how we should live the remaining years of our lives, and so we read and re-read the book of Revelation. Through this process, we wanted to unlearn ourselves of everything that had been taught previously about the book of Revelation. As Christians who believe the Bible, we put away all the preconceived notions about rapture and tribulation that we had heard and learned of, and absorbed every word of the Scripture, just like children learning the content for the first time.

No philosophy, no theology, no framework set by humans were to affect our reading; we only read in order to learn how we should live our lives during the last days of the world. During this time, we discovered many things in the Bible that were different from what we had learned. We also discovered that the book of Revelation was actually not as difficult as we had perceived before. And we believed in what our Lord has told us in the following verse:

[Rev 1:3] Blessed is he that readeth, and they that hear the words of this prophecy, and keep those things which are written therein: for the time is at hand.

We thought, if the book of Revelation was difficult to understand, our Lord could not speak to us as in Revelation 1:3. How can we read, hear, and keep what we do not understand? It was certain that our Lord has revealed Revelation in a manner that is easy for all to understand. Of course, this does not mean that we know or understand everything. Yet, we wished to learn as Lord's humble disciples and students.

Gradually, we saw the links between different parts of Revelation and the coherence of the links with other books of the Bible as well. We now wish to share what we have discovered with our readers.

We found that many events among the seven seals and seven trumpets in the book of Revelation have already occurred and are part of history already. We also found which incident in history each of the seven seals and five trumpets corresponds to. In this book series, we would like to share the evidences that suggest the correspondence of historical incidents to specific seals and trumpets, as well as the process it took to find the evidences.

We believe that those seals, trumpets, and bowls in Revelation are to be interpreted in chronological and sequential order. By sequential, we mean that the seals, the trumpets, and the bowls are to happen in the order they are written in the book of Revelation. By chronological, we mean that the events prophesied in the book of Revelation can be traced back in the human history, and that the sequence of the prophetic events would be fulfilled in the order of time.

As far as we know, no studies have been done on the seven seals in the light of past history as suggested in this book, although some scholars in the past had interpreted that Roman, Turkish, or other powers alike may have been related to the events of several seals and trumpets.

With the coming of Jesus ever so close, we could not find anyone who systematically interpreted that the seals, the trumpets, and the bowls were presented in the book of Revelation in a sequential order and that they actually occurred in chronological order in history. From our studies, we realized that in the present time we are about to witness the unfolding of the sixth trumpet, the Third World War. It is our wish that our readers may learn the imminence of the coming of our Lord and prepare themselves to meet Him.

We have also shared what the Lord has revealed to us (what we have discovered) on YouTube starting in 2010. The interpretations of the seven seals were uploaded from 2010 to 2012, and the seven trumpets in September of 2011. Afterwards, more detailed discourse on the book of Revelation has continued since May of 2013, including 68 lectures.

In the last chapter of Revelation, Jesus emphasizes His return by repeating the expression, "I come quickly," in three verses. So at this point we ask: How does the return of Jesus Christ affect us? Is there anything we should do about the return of Jesus Christ? Is there anything God wants us to do with regard to this matter? In fact, with the second coming of Jesus Christ detailed throughout the New Testament, we can easily find verses that guide what we as believers should do in preparation for His return.

Many of us live busily tending to daily affairs, and the busyness quite often makes the spiritual watchfulness or alertness we should maintain easily slip from our mind. Yet, the Bible emphasizes throughout the New Testament the pending return of Jesus Christ and the importance of believers' spiritual watchfulness and alertness that will enable them to stand before the Son of Man upon His return (Lk 21:36).

One may ask, "What is the point in knowing about the prophesied events if the world is bound to end anyway? If I live in ways acceptable and pleasing to God (1Th 2:4; 1Pe 2:5), isn't that enough?" Yet, our Lord reiterated about the last days that we should be watchful, look up, and lift up our heads (Mt 24:42; Lk 21:28). What does lifting up our heads mean? It means putting a stop to our preoccupation in the things of the earth and look up to things above in heaven and prepare for the return of our Lord.

[Eph 5:14] Wherefore he saith, Awake thou that sleepest, and arise from the dead, and Christ shall give thee light

With that said, it is our privilege to share our thought processes when it comes to interpreting the prophecies God has provided in the book of Revelation.

Andronicus Johnson, Caleb Lee, and Azaria Stephen

CHAPTER 1

SEQUENCE OF EVENTS
IN REVELATION

SEQUENTIAL ORDER OF EVENTS

This book series will primarily focus on the prophecies of events that must happen before the return of Jesus the Lord. Volume 1 will describe the seven seals. Volume 2 will go over the seven trumpets. And later volumes will discuss the appearance of the Antichrist and the wars he wages until the second coming of Jesus Christ.

Throughout history, many scholars and prophets have scrutinized the words in the book of Revelation and come up with their interpretations on the prophecy. As history continues to unveil the prophecies written in Revelation, it is important to constantly examine the legitimacy of the interpretations.

A basic, yet novel, approach to interpret the book of Revelation is introduced here: There are seven seals, seven trumpets, and seven bowls in Revelation. The seven seals, from the first to the seventh, are opened in a sequential order, then the seven trumpets from the first to the seventh are blown in a sequential order, and finally the seven bowls, again from the first to the last, are poured out sequentially. What is unique about this interpretation is that there are three different categories—seals, trumpets, and bowls—of events, and that they do not overlap in their timeline of occurrence.

Many have tried to understand the book of Revelation in order to know where mankind stands in the prophetic timeline. There are different interpretations with regard to the timeline today, and many of them imply that the events of seals, trumpets, and bowls occur without particular order.

But the book of Revelation is clearly written with the following purpose: to bless those who read, hear, and keep those things which are written in the prophecy (Rev 1:3). Here, the word *keep* in verse 3 comes from the Greek word τηρέω (*tēreō*), which means "to attend to carefully; to guard; to observe."[1] Thus, verse 3 translates as "anyone who observes or abides by the words of the book of Revelation is to be blessed" as promised by God.

To abide by the words of Revelation, however, one must have clear understanding of the written prophecies. Thus, if God wants to bless the readers, hearers, and observers, would He make the prophecies of Revelation so difficult that it is nearly impossible to interpret the sequence of the events laid out therein?

In Matthew 24:33, Jesus says, "So likewise ye, when ye shall see all these things, know that it is near, even at the doors," referring to the signs of Jesus' coming at the end of the age. Jesus Himself says in the Bible that disciples are to recognize and know the time as it nears His return to the earth. How are believers to recognize the time?

The answer is given in the Bible, especially in the book of Revelation, "the Revelation of Jesus Christ, which God gave unto him, to shew unto his servants things which must shortly come to pass" (Rev 1:1). And anyone who reads this book, hears this word, and abides by it is to know that the time is near and thereby able to prepare for the return of Jesus Christ. Thus, a rather simple approach to interpret the book of Revelation is pertinent: Interpret as literally as possible, and assume that seals are followed by trumpets, and then bowls follow trumpets in order. This approach is natural from a perspective that God wants His servants to know the nearing time of Jesus' return. He wants His servants to read and keep His words in Revelation because the time is near (Rev 1:3).

Consequently, God would have given Revelation in a way that the events therein and their sequence in time are easily identified and interpreted. In other words, Jesus wouldn't have made John write the book of Revelation in a way that would cause potential confusion or misunderstanding about the apocalyptic timeline.

Perhaps some may find this one-dimensional approach too simple. However, would God only allow those who are extraordinarily intelligent to interpret the prophetic timeline given in Revelation? It would be ironic if that were the case, since God blesses the one who reads, hears, and keeps those things which are written in Revelation. Anyone who is willing can read. Anyone who wills can hear. And anyone who wills shall abide by the word of God.

Thus, the seals, the trumpets, and the bowls occur in the order they are written in the book of Revelation. Assuming this is true, the prophetic events can now be matched to the corresponding historical incidents. If a historical incident were to be inferred as a prophetic event, such correlation can be established only if the definitive historical incident fulfills the description of the prophetic event written in Revelation.

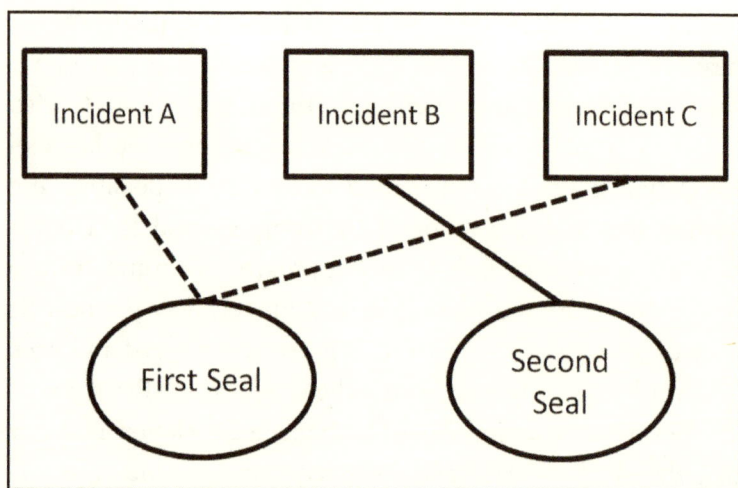

Fig. 1-1. Matching the historical incidents with the prophecies in Revelation. Incidents A and C are weakly coupled with the first seal, while incident B is almost certainly associated with the second seal. From this, the key reference point is now incident B as the second seal.

For further understanding, let there be three historical incidents, A, B, and C, in chronological order. Let us assume that the incidents A and C closely resemble the description of the first seal from Revelation. Let us also assume that the incident B unambiguously matches the description of the second seal. From this, conclusion is derived that the incident B refers to the second seal and that it serves as a chronological reference. From this, the incident C interpreted as the first seal should be ruled out, as it happened later than the incident B. In other words, with the help of chronological reference of the incident B, the first seal can be determined as the historical incident A rather than the incident C (refer to Fig. 1-1).

Like this, one prophetic event correctly identified in history can be used as a chronological landmark to identify other historical incidents as preceding or following prophetic events. Of course, the principle to follow is the sequence provided in Revelation. Such logic decreases chance of possible misinterpretation of prophetic events that could easily occur otherwise. Thus, it makes sense that the order of events written in Revelation is sequential; God wants believers to figure out the sequence easily, or with high probability of correctness.

Now, let's look at the seven trumpets and the seven bowls in detail.

As seen in Table 1-1, the first trumpet was sounded upon the *earth*, and the first bowl was also poured upon the *earth*. The second trumpet was sounded upon the *sea*, and the second bowl was also poured upon the *sea*. The third trumpet and the third bowl were upon the *rivers* and *fountains of waters*. The fourth trumpet and the fourth bowl were upon the *sun*. The fifth trumpet was sounded and a star that was given the key of the *bottomless pit* fell, and the fifth bowl was poured upon the seat of the *beast*. Since the beast is related to the bottomless pit, the fifth trumpet and bowl exhibit some relevance to each other. The sixth trumpet and the sixth bowl were both upon the *Euphrates River*. The seventh trumpet and the seventh bowl have common factors as well.

Some may think that with the common elements in each sequence of trumpets and bowls, the prophetic events of the same sequence would occur at the same time. However, the common elements in the trumpets and bowls are bona fide manifestation of God's sovereignty. They are, in fact, two discrete series of events, and are even designated with two distinct names—trumpets and bowls.

NO	TRUMPETS	BOWLS (VIALS) [2]
1	[Rev 8:7] The first angel sounded, and there followed hail and fire mingled with blood, and they were cast upon the *earth:* and the third part of trees was burnt up, and all green grass was burnt up.	[Rev 16:2] And the first went, and poured out his vial upon the *earth;* and there fell a noisome and grievous sore upon the men which had the mark of the beast, and upon them which worshipped his image.
2	[Rev 8:8] And the second angel sounded, and as it were a great mountain burning with fire was cast into the *sea:* and the third part of the sea became blood; [Rev 8:9] And the third part of the creatures which were in the sea, and had life, died; and the third part of the ships were destroyed.	[Rev 16:3] And the second angel poured out his vial upon the *sea;* and it became as the blood of a dead man: and every living soul died in the sea.

3	[Rev 8:10] And the third angel sounded, and there fell a great star from heaven, burning as it were a lamp, and it fell upon the third part of the *rivers*, and upon the *fountains of waters;* [Rev 8:11] And the name of the star is called Wormwood: and the third part of the waters became wormwood; and many men died of the waters, because they were made bitter.	[Rev 16:4] And the third angel poured out his vial upon the *rivers* and *fountains of waters;* and they became blood.
4	[Rev 8:12] And the fourth angel sounded, and the third part of the *sun* was smitten, and the third part of the moon, and the third part of the stars; so as the third part of them was darkened, and the day shone not for a third part of it, and the night likewise.	[Rev 16:8] And the fourth angel poured out his vial upon the *sun;* and power was given unto him to scorch men with fire.

5	[Rev 9:1] And the fifth angel sounded, and I saw a star fall from heaven unto the earth: and to him was given the key of the *bottomless pit.* [Rev 9:2] And he opened the bottomless pit; and there arose a smoke out of the pit, as the smoke of a great furnace; and the sun and the air were darkened by reason of the smoke of the pit.	[Rev 16:10] And the fifth angel poured out his vial upon the seat of the *beast*; and his kingdom was full of darkness; and they gnawed their tongues for pain,
6	[Rev 9:13] And the sixth angel sounded, and I heard a voice from the four horns of the golden altar which is before God, [Rev 9:14] Saying to the sixth angel which had the trumpet, Loose the four angels which are bound in the great river *Euphrates.* [Rev 9:15] And the four angels were loosed, which were prepared for an hour, and a day, and a month, and a year, for to slay the third part of men.	[Rev 16:12] And the sixth angel poured out his vial upon the great river *Euphrates;* and the water thereof was dried up, that the way of the kings of the east might be prepared.

| 7 | [Rev 11:15] And the seventh angel sounded; and there were great voices in heaven, saying, The kingdoms of this world are become the kingdoms of our Lord, and of his Christ; and he shall reign for ever and ever. [Rev 11:19] And the temple of God was opened in heaven, and there was seen in his temple the ark of his testament: and there were *lightnings*, and *voices*, and *thunderings*, and an *earthquake*, and *great hail*. | [Rev 16:17] And the seventh angel poured out his vial into the air; and there came a great voice out of the temple of heaven, from the throne, saying, It is done. [Rev 16:18] And there were *voices*, and *thunders*, and *lightnings;* and there was a *great earthquake*, such as was not since men were upon the earth, so mighty an earthquake, and so great. [Rev 16:21] And there fell upon men a *great hail* out of heaven, every stone about the weight of a talent: and men blasphemed God because of the plague of the hail; for the plague thereof was exceeding great. |

Table 1-1. Comparison of the verses describing seven trumpets versus seven bowls in the book of Revelation. Common disasters are italicized.

If trumpets were compared with bowls one by one sequentially, the seventh trumpet and the seventh bowl seem to share the most similarity between each other. However, closer examination of the seventh trumpet and the seventh bowl can lay a foundation for a point to be made. A lot of people have read the corresponding verses and concluded that the seventh trumpet and the seventh bowl must be the same event, the reason being, in the seventh trumpet, there are "lightnings," "voices," "thunders," an "earthquake," and "great hail," while in the seventh bowl, there are "voices," "thunders," "lightnings," a "great earthquake," and "great hail."

However, there is "a great earthquake" in the seventh bowl and merely "an earthquake" in the seventh trumpet. One adjective, *great*, surely makes a vast difference! Let's read Revelation 16:18, which describes the *great* earthquake of the seventh bowl: "There was a great earthquake, such as was not since men were upon the earth, so mighty an earthquake, and so great." This great earthquake, so mighty and unique that no earthquake like it was ever as seen before, is clearly a different one from the one in Revelation 11:19. Therefore, the seventh trumpet and the seventh bowl are not the same event.

If the seventh trumpet and the seventh bowl were the same event, then the prophetic timeline would have an overlap of the seventh trumpet and the seventh bowl. With this logic, figuring out which incident corresponds to which prophetic event in Revelation would turn into an enigmatic puzzle. This will cause many interpreters of the prophecy to come to different conclusions, resulting in great confusion. This is not a desirable phenomenon when it comes to interpreting Revelation.

It is only proper to believe that God, the author of Revelation, revealed the future in a manner minimizing any potential confusion in reaching a clear-cut interpretation. Only then, the reader, the listeners, and the observers of Revelation can prepare for the last days in accord with the Scriptures.

DISCLAIMER

It is important to note at this point that Jesus warns the disciples against trying to figure out the exact day and hour of His return.

[Mt 24:36] But of that day and hour knoweth no man, no, not the angels of heaven, but my Father only.

According to the Bible, only the Father God knows the exact timing of Jesus' return. However, many false prophets have emerged throughout the history and have announced the date and time of the end of the world or the return of Jesus. It should be clear here that predicting the exact day and/or hour of Jesus' return will not be attempted. Instead, by knowing the prophetic timeline today, all will be able to determine how to live according to the word of God.

With scientific development, available historical resources, and easy access to current incidents today, prophetic events in the book of Revelation are bound to be unveiled more clearly as time goes by. Today, some believe that the sixth seal is about to be opened. If that is true, then there will still be a lot of time left in the prophetic timeline until the return of Jesus.

However, the sixth seal is regarded as already having been opened in the past, and the sixth trumpet, soon to be sounding. If this is true, it means that there is far less time left until the return of the Lord Jesus Christ than one might expect. It is possible to foresee what incidents will occur in the near future based on the prophetic timeline. If indeed this is true, it is necessary for each to look into one's life and determine how to live the rest of it.

OCCURRENCE PATTERN OF THE PROPHETIC EVENTS

The sequence of the prophetic events has been defined in the order of seals, trumpets, and bowls provided in the book of Revelation. If that is the case and the prophecy is easy to understand, will everyone be aware of the second coming of Jesus and be preparing for His return? The Bible indicates that is not the case. The events in the prophetic timeline will be fulfilled suddenly, like "a thief in the night," as 1 Thessalonians 5:2 describes. This is also warned of in verse 3:

[1 Th 5:3] For when they shall say, Peace and safety; then sudden destruction cometh upon them, as travail upon a woman with child; and they shall not escape.

Here, "they" represent the unbelievers, and possibly Christians spiritually asleep as well, and to them the destruction will come suddenly. In other words, "they" will be living their days thinking that the world is in such peace and safety, and will have nowhere to escape upon sudden end of the age. Verse 4, however, says that the believers following the Christ will not be suddenly overtaken by the destruction.

[1 Th 5:4] But ye, brethren, are not in darkness, that that day should overtake you as a thief.

This shows that through God's mercy towards His children, believers shall know the imminence of His coming by observing His word.

How would the prophetic events occur one after another? Would the second seal be opened immediately after the first seal is opened? Would a trumpet be sounded immediately after its previous trumpet? Would it be the same for the bowls? In order to answer such questions, the word of God should be sought after, rather than mere assumptions be made.

Throughout Revelation, there are verses that describe time lapse between certain prophetic events. Revelation 9:12 writes, "One woe is past; and behold, there come two woes more hereafter." As Revelation 9:1–11 discuss the fifth trumpet, the first woe is undoubtedly referring to the *fifth trumpet*. The second and third woes refer to the sixth and seventh trumpets, respectively. Revelation 9:12 implies that there is a period of time after the fifth trumpet is sounded and before the sixth and seventh trumpets are sounded. Likewise, the following verse depicts a certain period of time that will pass prior to the *third woe*, the seventh trumpet, after the sixth trumpet is sounded:

[Rev 11:14] The second woe is past; and, behold, the third woe cometh quickly.

This implies that events in Revelation can occur with a certain lapse of time in between. In other words, the Bible demonstrates that prophetic events do not always occur immediately one after another, but that the events may follow a certain time after their previous ones.

The Bible provides a very specific description of the prophetic timeline, as in 1 Thessalonians 5:3. According to the Scripture, the sudden destruction comes as travail upon a woman with child. This travail, or labor pains of a pregnant woman, becomes "more frequent, intense, and regular" over time until delivery.[3] The events that lead to destruction then must come initially in relatively low frequency, which will increase as His return draws near.

Based on the Scriptures, it can be assumed that each seal is opened after many years passed since the previous seal, for instance, over centurial intervals; each trumpet is sounded after much shorter period of time has elapsed, over decadal intervals between trumpets; and each bowl is poured within shortest span of time. All the bowls are to be poured at the second half of the last seven years, found in chapter 16 of Revelation. In other words, the seven bowls are to be poured out within 3.5 years, which reduces the interval between each bowl into less than a year. This is the generalized sequential pattern that one may expect to see as the prophetic events unfold. The following verses illustrate this pattern:

[Rev 8:1] And when he had opened the seventh seal, there was silence in heaven about the space of half an hour.

[Rev 8:2] And I saw the seven angels which stood before God; and to them were given seven trumpets.

[Rev 8:5] And the angel took the censer, and filled it with fire of the altar, and cast it into the earth: and there were voices, and thunderings, and lightnings, and an earthquake.

The verses display the seventh seal as well as the preparation of the seven trumpets. Verse 1 shows that the seventh seal is opened. In verse 2, John sees God giving the seven trumpets to seven angels. In verse 5, the seventh seal is carried out. Why are all the trumpets prepared between the opening and the execution of the seventh seal? Why isn't only a single event, for example, the first trumpet, prepared as the seventh seal is about to be executed? A possible reason is that the average interval between seals might be comparable to the period of all seven trumpets combined. In other words, the intervals between seals are far longer than those of trumpets.

In sum, the intervals of the events have the tendency of getting shortened over time, similar to the above-mentioned metaphor of the labor pains of a pregnant woman.

Based on the Holy Scriptures, it is established that seals, trumpets, and bowls occur in sequential order without overlaps. It is postulated that: The times at which the seals are opened are spread throughout centuries; after all seven of the seals have been opened, the first trumpet is sounded; then the following trumpets are sounded in intervals of decade(s); after all seven of the trumpets are sounded, seven bowls are poured within a few years in order. It is important to remember that these events do not necessarily occur immediately after each previous event.

CHAPTER 2

THE FOURTH SEAL:
KILL WITH DEATH AND BEASTS

THE MOST EASILY IDENTIFIABLE SEAL

Let us now discuss the seven seals in the book of Revelation. In the book of Revelation, there are seven seals, seven trumpets, and seven bowls. Jesus said that these events will happen like the labor pain of a pregnant woman. What is the labor pain like? It comes once in a while in the beginning. Then it becomes more frequent as time goes by and the baby grows in the womb. When it nears time for the woman to give birth, labor pain comes in much accelerated frequency and possibly in higher intensity.

Likewise, it is expected that the interval between each seal is longer, compared to that of trumpets or bowls, since the seals are opened prior to the trumpets or the bowls. If the intervals of the seals are in the order of centuries, as it has been almost two millennial years since Revelation was written, at least some of the seals must have been opened. After going through this presentation, it will become clear that all of the seals have actually opened, that they have been correctly identified in history, and that the coming of the Lord Jesus is near. These facts should challenge anyone to be alert and awake to His return.

The simplest way to interpret the seals is to first look for the event that seems most easily identifiable. After such seal is identified with respect to history, then its previous or following seal can be identified based on this interpretation. For example, if the first seal happened in the year 500, then the second seal would have happened after 500, and so on.

Out of all seven seals, seven trumpets, and seven bowls, the seventh events always consist of voices, thunderings, lightnings, and earthquake (refer to Table 1-1). When three events result in same disasters, although the intensity may differ, it would be very difficult to identify the seventh seal.

For example, let's assume a time in history that has been identified, during which there were voices, thunderings, lightnings, and earthquake present. What could assure that the derived interpretation pertains to the seventh seal, the seventh trumpet, or the seventh bowl? Due to the difficulty involved with the task, it is better to avoid the seventh seal as a starting point of research.

Out of six seals, the most easily identifiable seal would be an event that is cataclysmic or regarded as historically significant in the grand scheme of things. If it were a very peculiar event, then it would be easily identified. Out of the six seals, it seems that the fourth seal would have been a very compelling incident in history. Here is the passage of Scripture pertaining to the fourth seal:

[Rev 6:7] And when he had opened the fourth seal, I heard the voice of the fourth beast say, Come and see.

[Rev 6:8] And I looked, and behold a pale horse: and his name that sat on him was Death, and Hell followed with him. And power was given unto them over the fourth part of the earth, to kill with sword, and with hunger, and with death, and with the beasts of the earth.

In the passage above, the impact of the fourth seal reaches the fourth part of "the earth." This indicates that the history would have recorded this event with a high number of deaths.

But before moving on to identify this event, it must be pointed out that the phrase "the earth" (τῆς γῆς, *tēs gēs*) may signify the region impacted by this event or the entire planet Earth. This is because the expression "the earth" includes the definite article "the" (τῆς, *tēs*), which may render a limiting effect, confining the region to the area of pertinence only. If so, it might imply that the power was given to the rider over only the fourth part of the region this event had occurred. On the contrary, if "the earth" represents the whole planet, then the event would have affected the fourth part of Earth.

The Scripture says that after the fourth seal is opened, there is a pale horse with Death and Hell accompanying it. In the original text in Greek, the word "Hell" here is ᾅδης which reads *hadēs*, and has the following meaning: "1) name Hades or Pluto, the god of the lower regions; 2) Orcus, the nether world, the realm of the dead; 3) later use of this word: the grave, death, hell."[1] According to the prophecy, Death and Hell have power over the fourth part of the earth, and with that power, they kill with sword, hunger, death, and beasts of the earth.

The word "hunger" is translated from the original Greek word, λιμός, which reads *limos* and means "scarcity of harvest, famine."[2] So according to the prophecy in original Greek text, when the fourth seal opened, many people were killed, whether due to sword, *famine*, death, or beasts of the earth. And if these events had already happened, surely history would have left mark of their death toll and tragedy.

Thus, to interpret the fourth seal, incidents in history that coincide with the descriptions of the prophecy are searched. In other words, since the fourth seal consists of four major descriptions of events that caused death of people over the fourth part of the earth, four particular incidents in history are expected to have resulted in a high death toll.

The premise is that the book of Revelation provides a chronological sequence in which the prophetic events occur. Historical incidents that killed many people are searched in the following order: sword, famine, death, and then beasts of the earth, just as written in the prophecy.

In other words, if these four events in the prophecy of the fourth seal are to occur in chronological order, then a high death toll that was caused by "the beasts of the earth" would have occurred at a particular time. A high death toll caused by "death" would be observed prior to the death by "the beasts of the earth." Likewise, "famine" would have caused a high death toll before "death," and the "sword" earlier than "famine."

In order to search for the historical incidents that are associated with these prophetic events of the fourth seal, the first research conducted was regarding the "beasts of the earth."

WITH DEATH, AND WITH THE BEASTS OF THE EARTH

The incident in which many were killed by "beasts of the earth" would have happened after the incident in which many were killed by "death." However, a question arose as an attempt was made to identify historical incidents in relation to the prophecy of the fourth seal.

It was rather unclear that one of the methods that Death and Hades use to kill was "death," while the remaining three methods provided clear, specific causes that led to death. Here, "to kill with sword" can well mean that people die from the blades of swords. "To kill with hunger" also could indicate that people die from extreme hunger or famine. "To kill with the beasts of the earth" would mean that in one way or another, wild beasts will kill men. But "to kill with death"—how much more vague and uncertain can the meaning be?

Confused by the text, the meaning of the word "death" was surveyed in the original Greek. Upon scrutinizing the Scripture, another meaning for "death" was found: "pestilence."[3] This definition has actually been well supported by various Bible commentaries, some of which shall be briefly examined at this point.

According to the *Vincent's Word Studies* commentary, "The Hebrew *deber*, *pestilence*, is rendered by the Greek word for *death* in the Septuagint."[4] *Adam Clarke's Commentary on the Bible* also states that "death" here refers to pestilence.[5]

The following is an excerpt from *Albert Barnes' Notes on the Bible*, which also states that "death" in Revelation 6:8 most likely refers to pestilence, one of the usual outcomes of war:

> *And with death* – Each of the other forms – "with the sword and with hunger" – imply that death would reign; for it is said that "power was given to kill with sword and with hunger." This word, then, must refer to death in some other form – to death that seemed to reign without any such visible cause as the "sword" and

"hunger." This would well denote the pestilence – not an infrequent accompaniment of war. For nothing is better suited to produce this than the unburied bodies of the slain; the filth of a camp; the want of food; and the crowding together of multitudes in a besieged city; and, accordingly, the pestilence, especially in Oriental countries, has been often closely connected with war. That the pestilence is referred to here is rendered more certain by the fact that the Hebrew word רבד (*deber*), "pestilence," which occurs about fifty times in the Old Testament, is rendered θάνατος *thanatos*, "death," more than thirty times in the Septuagint.[6]

Barnes' last sentence, which states that the Hebrew word "pestilence" in the Old Testament was frequently translated as "death" in the Septuagint, certainly adds much to the conviction that the mortality caused by "death" (Rev 6:8) might have been due to pestilence. Conclusively, these commentaries seem to point to the fact that the word "death" in Revelation 6:8 actually refers to pestilence.

If "death" (Rev 6:8) was written to actually mean "pestilence," then the "beasts of the earth" (Rev 6:8) may have contributed to the event related to "death" (Rev 6:8), as the meaning of the word "pestilence" includes "bubonic plague," infection "transmitted by fleas from infected rodents."[7, 8]

Furthermore, the fact that Death and Hades have power over "the fourth part of the earth" to "kill" with "the beasts of the earth" signifies that the population of those killed by the beasts was probably not restricted to a local region or one nation, but across a vast land area, or several nations at least. Also, it is probably more likely that humans fell victim to contagious spread of a disease carried by the wild beasts rather than directly being attacked in physical manner over a large area.

There is another interesting twist of language in the original Greek text of Revelation 6:8 that indicates "death" and "beasts of the earth" are a common event in killing many people. Revelation 6:8 states: "to kill with sword, and with hunger, and with death, and with the beasts of the earth." Notice that the word "with" is used in front of each causative agents used to kill—sword, hunger, death, and beasts of the earth. In the original Greek text, the "with" in front of "sword," "hunger," and "death" is ἐν (*en*), and means "in, by, with, etc."[9] However, the "with" used in front of "beasts of the earth" is not ἐν (*en*), but ὑπό (*hypo*), and means "by, under."[10] The original Scripture, therefore, reads, "And power was given unto them over the fourth part of the earth, to kill with sword, and with hunger, and with pestilence and by the beasts of the earth" (Rev 6:8b). Thus, the mortalities caused by "beasts of the earth" and by "death" in Revelation 6:8 might actually be of the same event.

To understand what the significance of this difference in words may be, let us now read some of the excerpts from various commentaries of the Bible. According to *A Commentary on the Old and New Testaments* by Robert Jamieson, A. R. Fausset and David Brown, the word "with" used in front of "beasts of the earth" means "by" in Greek, indicating "more direct agency" of the beasts in the killing of many people.[11]

The *Vincent's Word Studies* commentary states:

> *With the beasts* (ὑπὸ τῶν θηρίων, *hypo tōn thēriōn*): Rev.,
> *by.* The preposition ὑπό (*hypo*) *by* is used here instead of
> ἐν (*en*) *in* or *with*, indicating more definitely *the actual*

agent of destruction; while ἐν (*en*) denotes the *element* in which the destruction takes place, and gives a general indication of the manner in which it was wrought.[12]

Both commentaries seem to suggest that the "with" in front of "beasts of the earth" was written to indicate the beasts as a direct causative agent in killing many.

The word "death" (Rev 6:8) may be read as "pestilence," and pestilence is associated with bubonic plague transmitted by fleas and rodents. Perhaps the "beasts" (Rev 6:8) was written to provide a specific clue on the cause of "death" – pestilence transmitted by wild animals or "beasts of the earth." With this possibility in mind, the search began for the most probable or expected pestilence incident in history that would have had earthly beasts or wild animals killing many people.

THE BLACK DEATH IN EUROPE

One of the greatest pestilences in human history is the Black Death, which peaked between 1348 and 1350.[13] This bubonic plague is known as one of the most devastating plague pandemics in history.

The infection is known to have been carried by Oriental rat fleas living on black rats that traveled on merchant ships throughout the Mediterranean and Europe. These black rats, most likely the "beasts of the earth" mentioned in the prophecy of the fourth seal, carried the fleas that acted as the medium for spreading the infection caused by *Yersinia pestis* bacteria.[14] This strain of bacteria originated from China[15] and spread throughout Europe, causing the reduction of Europe's population by approximately 30 to 60 percent from 1348 to 1420.[16, 17]

Dr. Justus Hecker, a professor in Germany who conducted an extensive work of research on the Black Death wrote a book entitled *The Epidemics of the Middle Ages* in the year 1832. In it, he estimated that in total, a fourth part of the inhabitants of Europe were carried off by the plague.[18]

According to Dr. Hecker, Giovanni Boccaccio witnessed the pandemic in Florence. In his testimony, he described how gruesome the effects of pandemic were:

> The plague spread itself with the greater fury, as it communicated from the sick to the healthy, like fire among dry and oily fuel, and even contact with the clothes and other articles which had been used by the infected seemed to induce the disease. As it advanced, not only men, but animals, fell sick and shortly expired, if they had touched things belonging to the diseased or dead.[19]

Similar scenes, signs, and symptoms were observed throughout various affected regions, such as Egypt, Germany, Austria, Westphalia, France, England, Sweden, Norway, Poland, Russia, and others.[20]

Based on these facts, testimonies, and estimations, the Black Death that peaked between 1348 and 1350, reducing Europe's population drastically, is one of the fulfilled events of the fourth seal. The Black Death fulfills the description of the fourth seal due to the nature of disease, as it caused "death" through pestilence by "beasts of the earth," rodents and fleas.

Lastly, let us briefly go over another interesting use of the word "beasts" in the original Greek text of Revelation 6:8. Usually the word "beasts" reminds people of large, monstrous animals. In fact, the word "beast" is defined as "any nonhuman animal, especially a large, four-footed mammal" and its synonyms include "cad, swine, pig, brute, savage, ogre, monster, [and] barbarian."[21]

So if "beasts" in Revelation 6:8 actually referred to such large, four-footed mammals, interpreting the Black Death, which was spread by fleas on rats, as a part of the fourth seal would be absolutely unreasonable. However, the word "beast" in its original text in Greek originates from the word θηρίον, transliterated as *thērion*. This word is actually a diminutive form of the root word θήρ, transliterated as *thēr*, which means "a wild animal"."[22] Hence, the word "beast" or θηρίον (*thērion*) in Revelation 6:8 originally means "a little beast, little animal,"[23] although it cannot be ignored that it has been translated in various places in the Bible mostly to signify "beast," "wild beast," and "venomous beast." Also the "beast" many times represents the Antichrist.[24]

Thus, the fact that "beasts" can actually be referring to "little beasts" further enhances the proposition that the Black Death, a bubonic plague caused by infected fleas and rats, is part of the prophesied events of the fourth seal.

According to the fourth seal, power was given over the fourth part of the earth. It would be more appropriate to interpret it as the power over the earth extended to the fourth part of its area, rather than to say that fourth part of the people living on the earth were killed by the bubonic plague. Therefore, just as it is important to examine how many people had died, it is just as important to review how much area of the earth was affected.

History shows that the bubonic plague/the Black Death did not occur in a small corner of some remote township but over a large area all across Europe and Asia. If the power over the fourth part of the earth does not refer to death of fourth of mankind but to the power to affect the people in that particular fourth part of the land area, then the "earth" in the passage probably refers to the entire globe.

In this regard, whether the event of the fourth seal has affected the fourth part of Earth should be examined. The fact that many people have died must be verified also, since the Scripture reveals that the rider's name is Death, and Hell followed with him. The number of deaths caused by the Black Death from Europe and a part of Russia alone is sufficient to state that the fourth seal is a global event and has opened already. Therefore, further research was conducted to check if the plague has occurred in any area outside of European perimeter.

PLAGUES IN CHINA AND INDIA

It is time to verify whether a significant portion of Earth was indeed affected by the plague. Since it is already a well-known fact that many people died in Europe and a part of Russia from bubonic plague, now the areas of Middle East, China, and India need substantiated evidence to confirm whether the plague pandemic was present in those regions, if so, when was the peak time of the Black Death, and its influence on the number of casualties.

The Black Death is considered one of the biggest natural disasters in human history. Wherever the plague had spread, it depopulated the regions by 25 percent to 50 percent. Studies show that there is no mistake in stating that the plague had been spread to Constantinople via the Mongol invasion, to the west in the 1340s.[25] Scientists have recently shown that the plague-causing pathogenic strain *Yersinia pestis* had originated from China through DNA analysis.[26]

Studies also show that the pathogen was passed from China to Constantinople, where the Genoese traders got infected, through whom the plague spread to Europe and Northern Africa.[27] In other words, the Black Death not only caused many deaths in Europe but also in Asia and Northern Africa.

But the plague peaked in Asia later than in Europe as the following ABC News program reported about the Black Death:

> The Black Death also devastated the Middle East, reaching Antioch in 1348-49, Mecca and Mosul in 1349, and Yemen in 1351 . . . The successive pandemics caused massive depopulation. In China, some two-thirds of the population died in eight geographically separate incidents from 1353 to 1354, after 90% of the people in Hubei had died in the initial outbreak. In Europe, some 70% of the people had died from the Black Plague by 1400 . . . In Damascus, some 25-40% of the people died, with 1,000 dying horribly each day at the peak of the outbreak. The Black Death was many things, but it was not unique to Europe, and did not start there – it came from China.[28]

Let us further investigate the lethality of the Black Death when it peaked in China. In 1353, areas such as Hupeh, Kiangsi, Shansi, and Suiyuan were affected, and especially in Shansi, more than two-thirds of people died. And by 1354, regions of Shansi, Hupeh, Hopei, Kiangsi, Hunan, Kwangtung, and Kwangsi were reported with plague, and especially in Hupeh, the fatality reached 60 percent to 70 percent of its population.[29]

From these observations, despite *Yersinia pestis* having originated from China, the Black Death peaked in China from

1353 to 1354, which is later than the Black Death's peak in Europe between 1348 and 1350. Likewise, it seems the Black Death peaked in the Middle East a bit later than Europe as well.

Fig. 2-1. Spread of the Black Death in 1351.[30]

In sum, as shown in the map (refer to Fig. 2-1), the Black Death caused fatality throughout Asia including the Middle East, Europe, and Northern Africa. The broad coverage befits the fourth seal's prophetic description on the fourth part of planet Earth.

But at this point, it is necessary to verify whether the plague had spread in India. It is unclear when the plague was introduced to India. Unfortunately, a record of the plague in India is non-existent from that time. Despite the non-existence, many argue out of speculation that the plague had started in China and transferred to Europe via India. However, some recent theses conclude that such speculative argument that the plague had transit through India lacks credibility and is unfounded, because the Western scholars at the time did not consult India's historic records.

With regard to this, let us review what Sussman published in the *Bulletin of the History of Medicine:* "But a close examination of the sources on the Delhi Sultanate . . . provides no evidence of any serious epidemic in fourteenth-century India . . ."[31]

Another source concludes:

Support for the claim that the Black Death visited India before it spread to Europe comes from the chronicles of medieval merchants of Venice and Genoa, medieval historians from the Middle East, and other chroniclers of Europe. Gabriele de' Mussi, a thirteenth-century chronicler from Piacenza, wrote an account of the Black Death in which he mentioned that almost everyone in the East, including the population of India, was affected by the pestilence. An anonymous Flemish cleric wrote that in Greater India it rained frogs, serpents, lizards, scorpions and many venomous beasts and, on the third day, the whole province was infected. It should be noted that when a medieval merchant from Venice or Genoa refers to Greater India, he is referring to the region bounded by Central Asia in the north and Indonesia in the south . . . There appears to be no evidence from Indian sources to support the assertion that there was a plague in India in the fourteenth century. It is likely that merchant chroniclers who traveled along the Silk Road witnessed and wrote about the plague that was ravaging parts of Asia, north of India. What they meant by India in their chronicles is probably not part of India now.[32]

These indications alone cannot affirm that plague afflicted India; therefore, the illustrative map only represents the speculative work of the Western scholars. It is certain that there is no historic record evidencing the plague during this period in India. Naturally, India needs to be excluded from the total area affected.

Perhaps the area referred as India by the Western sources in the fourteenth century is Central and Southern Asia, the west and south of China, and not necessarily the India as it is today. And it is likely that China, not today's India, suffered the plague during the period based on the Western records at that time.

POPULATION REDUCTION IN THE AFFECTED LAND

As a result of such a tremendous blow from the plague, the population of Europe was reduced significantly and "it took roughly 200 years for Europe's population to regain its 1340 level."[33] In 1340, the world population was 443 million, but by 1400 it was reduced to between 350 to 374 million, possibly due to the Black Death.[34] Over time, the infection spread and reached the populations in Asia, Europe, and Africa. In other words, it can be speculated that the Black Death influenced the world population reduction by 16 percent to 21 percent in all. It shows how widely the plague had spread in accordance with the prophecy of the fourth seal that writes about the rider "Death," whom Hell followed to kill people with the pestilence.

Now it is time to calculate the Black Death's impact over the total land area. The Black Death had covered Europe, most of Asia, North Africa, and a part of Russia. Since no historical record from India or other sources from that time period substantiate the presence of the plague, India will be excluded from the calculation of total affected region, as some scholars confirmed that any previous reference to India as an affected region was nothing but an unfounded, speculative work. Also, with regard to Eastern Europe, although a part of Russia was under the plague's influence, the majority of Russia was intact from the plague. The area free from the plague, the east side of Asia and a portion of Europe, may cancel out the area affected in parts of Northern Africa and parts of Russia, as those areas may be deemed equal in coverage.

In sum, subtracting the land area of India ($3,287,590$ km^2) and Russia ($17,098,242$ km^2) from the total area of Asia ($44,579,000$ km^2) plus Europe ($10,180,000$ km^2) would yield the approximate calculation of the affected area by the plague. Therefore, the total area that had fallen under the bubonic plague comes out to be $44,579,000$ km^2 – $3,287,590$ km^2 – $17,098,242$ km^2 + $10,180,000$ km^2 = $34,373,168$ km^2.

Also, while the Earth's total land area is $148,940,000$ km^2, the uninhabitable Antarctica region amounts to $14,000,000$ km^2.[35, 36] Therefore, subtracting the uninhabitable Antarctic region from the Earth's total land area would yield the total habitable land area which is $148,940,000$ km^2 – $14,000,000$ km^2 = $134,940,000$ km^2.

Consequently, the percentage of total area affected by the Black Death comes out to be $34,373,168$ / $134,940,000$ = 0.255 = 25.5%. This calculation is obviously a mere estimation. Nonetheless, it clearly signifies that "the fourth part of Earth" was indeed affected by the Black Death.

CHAPTER 3

THE FOURTH SEAL: KILL WITH HUNGER

THE GREAT EUROPEAN FAMINE

Since the killing of many with "death" and "beasts of the earth" by Death and Hell in Revelation 6:8 was fulfilled through the Black Death, which peaked from 1348 to 1350, killing of many with "hunger" would have to have been fulfilled prior to 1348.

As previously mentioned, the word "hunger" in Revelation 6:8 is translated from the original Greek word, "λιμός" (*limos*), meaning "scarcity of harvest, famine."[1] Thus, the search for the incident that corresponds to the killing of many by the means of famine and the resultant hunger was rather simple; "great famines" that occurred throughout mankind's history were examined.

It was relatively easy to find an incident named the Great Famine that occurred from 1315 to 1317, which seemed to be an incident consistent with the timeline since it occurred during a time period right before the Black Death occurred.

A scholar named Henry S. Lucas had gathered and organized details of the Great European Famine of 1315–1317 into an article in the journal *Speculum* in 1930, which was published by the Medieval Academy of America. In his article, *The Great European Famine of 1315, 1316, and 1317,* he describes famine and pestilence that afflicted the European population during the fourteenth century as major phenomena that characterize the period.[2]

Overall, the Great European Famine is known to have affected a large area of Europe, the boundaries reaching as far west as the mountain range of Pyrenees, which borders France and Spain, as far east as the plains in Russia, north as far as Scotland, and south as far as Italy. This famine practically had its coverage over entire Europe, excluding only a few countries. Sir Lucas' report, which, according to his own words, was written "to give a more living picture of this most extraordinary catastrophe," provides the rather shocking details of the European society before, during, and after it was hit by the Great European Famine.[3]

The major cause of the famine was the peculiarly abundant number of torrential rainfalls that persisted and destroyed cropland and soil throughout Europe, the economy of which was primarily agrarian. Thus, this famine was a natural disaster, something that the Europeans could not control or fight against directly but could only strive to survive through any means possible.[4] The great famine struck the European societies in the early fourteenth century, devastating their economies, health, and morality, as a result.

The catastrophic effects of the famine were intensified by the fact that the European societies were mainly agrarian and relied on local farmers for food supplies. Also, people in the cities had not yet developed a custom of storing foods in case of shortage or disaster and relied on rural areas for food products. With population growth, the demand for food was higher than local supplies could meet, but importing activities were not as active. All of these conditions in the European societies exacerbated the effects of the great rainfalls that led to a long, painful period of famine. With the sudden onset of famine came decline and poverty in Europe.[5]

The Great European Famine was caused by torrential downpours throughout the continent. In England, an inundating rain started on May 11, 1315, around Pentecost, and did not stop until the fall. In France, rainfall started in April of 1315. Germany is known to have suffered from severe rainfall as well. The Low Countries of present-day Belgium, Netherlands, Luxembourg, and parts of France and Germany where the rainfall started in early May are estimated to have been under greater influence than other affected regions. Belgium, Netherlands and Holland had their low lands submerged in rainwater that washed away dikes and damaged croplands, causing tremendous environmental and social effects.[6]

Armies could not advance in war due to lands changing into bogs. Most forms of trade and transport stopped for similar reasons. Wagons would not budge, stuck in wet ground, even with the forces of several horses pulling together. Crop fields were obviously destroyed, as the water rotted seeds in wet ground and drowned plants. The years of the Great European Famine reaped poor harvest, if any, and people suffered from extreme hunger. Such was the rainy, cloudy, cold and out-of-control weather seen in "most of Europe north of the Alps."[7]

Many crops and food, including wine, almost stopped being produced for sale. According to Sir Lucas, wine production in France was poor in both quantity and quality due to lack of sunlight accompanied with incessant rainfall. The clouded sky, lowered temperature, and reduced sunlight all contributed to minimal harvest.[8]

As a result, wine commerce of France and Germany with neighboring countries hardly remained. Salt became unobtainable because it simply could not be evaporated from seawater throughout European countries. Grains, such as wheat, rye, oats, barley, spelt, and corn, did not fully grow during the cold, muddy summer, and could not be properly sown under this condition, and even if they survived, failed to ripen in time of harvest. Such were the outcomes of grain production in England, Ireland, France, Germany, and others.[9]

Market prices of food skyrocketed with the immediate downturn of European economies. Domestic animals also suffered from famine, which led to reduction of edible meat. Sir Lucas reported regarding the European market prices of various foods during the famine: "From these facts it is evident that there was universal failure of crops in 1315 in most if not all the lands of Europe from the Pyrenees to Slavic regions, from Scotland to Italy."[10]

As people found themselves unable to properly nourish themselves with just the scarce amount of grain available, they fed themselves dung of doves, leaves and roots, dead animals infected with pests, and even their own children. Hungry prisoners, with no food provided, attacked and ate newly arrived prisoners. Mothers survived by eating their own children and men ate bodies dug out of graves. Mortality skyrocketed as theft, robbery, burglary, vagabondage, violence, assault, murder, and other public crimes became common.[11]

According to Sir Lucas, "persons who ordinarily led a decent and respectable life were forced into irregularities of conduct which made them criminals." Anything was stolen, from "cattle, sheep, horses, hares, rabbits, partridges, pheasants, deer, and corn" to "hay, timber, stones, lead." "In fact all things of value were readily taken." With dead bodies and starving people everywhere throughout Europe, perhaps demoralization was an inevitable consequence.[12]

In England, King Edward II ordered that the coastlines be guarded against villains who frequently attacked, killed, and robbed foods and goods from merchants and fishermen who arrived at the seashore. In Paris, people found inedible materials such as "the dregs of wine and the dung of hogs" mixed into breads sold by bakeries. As a result, "A salutary punishment was imposed: sixteen offenders were placed on wheels in the public places of the town and were forced to hold in their raised hands fragments of the rotten bread. They were thereupon banished from the country."[13]

Malnourished from famine, people were highly vulnerable to pathogens and suffered from diseases and pestilences of various kinds. Commonly suffered diseases included "dysentery, high fever, and a fetid infection of the throat." People, probably those who were exposed to infected grain or grain products, developed erysipelas, or St. Anthony's fire, a skin disease induced by a micro-organism. Anthrax, great murrain, and other infections rapidly killed citizens, as infections spread from plants and animals to people who consumed them.[14]

According to Sir Lucas, "the number of the dead was so great in many places that there were not enough persons sufficiently well to bury them." People died away no matter what socioeconomic class they belonged to. Rich or poor, educated or non-educated, they all suffered from pestilence and died.[15]

FAMINES IN CHINA AND INDIA

There is no doubt the Great European Famine caused Europe much death and desolation. Now, it should be investigated if famine had occurred during the same period in other regions, especially in Asia, to see if the Great European Famine of 1315–1317 indeed is only a part of the prophesied event in Revelation 6:8, "hunger" that killed "over the fourth part of the earth," a vast portion of the world.

It is not farfetched to think the probability would be low to have such large-scale famine that devastated nearly all Europe would have also appeared in Asia during the same period. Considering that the Scripture of the fourth seal mentions "hunger" prior to "death," the famine clearly has to have occurred before the Black Death. And the likelihood of history revealing itself in such order of occurrence may not necessarily be high. If accounting for Europe alone, there is a probable chance; however, to include China into the equation, the probability lessens quickly.

In Europe, the Great European Famine occurred in 1315 which is earlier than 1348, when the Black Death had spread. But is this the case for China and India? Research below shows that the rare possibility of having European, Asian, and Indian regions experiencing an extensive famine before the Black Death had actually been a reality. Both historical phenomena affected a vast portion of Earth—"over the fourth part of the earth!"

Under the section titled *Chinese famine which started the Black Death* in an article published in the *National Geographic* magazine, a famine in China was discussed:

China is another land which famine seems to have marked for its own. Here the difficulty is not so much a matter of crop failures as the excess production of the human crop from year to year. Existence is a perpetual struggle for food in the Celestial Empire, and the smallest deviation from a maximum yield destroys the margin of safety between "barely enough" and "starvation." The four years between 1333 and 1337 constituted a period of unimagined suffering throughout China, and it is highly probable that it was in this era that the seeds of disaster were sown for Europe's Black Death, which appeared in the following decade. Famine and pestilence laid the whole country waste. Excessive rains caused destructive inundations, and according to Chinese records 4,000,000 people perished from starvation in the neighborhood of Kiang alone. Violent earthquakes occurred in many parts of the kingdom; whole mountains were thrown up and vast lakes formed. The fury of the elements subsided and the ravages of famine ceased in the very year that the Black Death reached England.[16]

In sum, the famine in China contributed to the start of the plague in Europe.

Another section titled *Famine's terrible toll in India* discusses Indian famine as follows:

In the ancient chronicles of Indian courts little space is given to the sufferings [of] the common people; hence the early accounts of famine are meager; but occasionally a single sentence from a poem or a historical sketch is illuminating in its very brevity. For example, we find the line, "The flesh of a son was preferred to his love," grimly suggesting the practice of cannibalism in times of dearth . . . while at about the time that the Black Death was making its appearance in Europe a famine of such severity swept over Hindustan . . .[17]

The famine in India during this period refers to 1335–1342, and the records show it had impacted the Northern India, including Delhi.[18] Other records reveal the famine that had started in 1344 continued for years, decimating the population of Doab.[19] From 1344 to 1345, India suffered "the Great Famine," and even the emperor and his family could not escape hunger. With the famine lasting for years, the death toll due to starvation reached millions. In summary, this famine had begun in 1335 and reached its peak intensity between 1344 and 1345.[20]

Any list of famines available from an encyclopedia would yield the Great European Famine of 1315–1317, Famine of China from 1333 to 1337, and the Great Famine of India from 1344 to 1345, in this chronological sequence![21]

The Great European Famine affected vast regions, including parts of Russia.[22] Research confirmed the famine had not only swept through Europe and Russia, but also China and India as well, before the Black Death peaked in Europe in 1348.

In case of China, the plague had peaked in 1353 to 1354 while the famine had occurred from 1333 to 1337. Thus, the famine had appeared prior to the plague. In case of India, the famine had occurred from 1335 to 1345.

The regions affected by the extensive famines share common regions impacted by the Black Death, but they are not entirely the same. As discussed previously, the famine that began in China from 1333 to 1337 probably contributed to the emergence of the Black Death in Europe by increasing the vulnerability of people to the virulence of the Black Death in the commonly affected regions. Being contagious in origin, the pestilence spread throughout a quarter of Earth.

Each area killed with "sword," "hunger," and "death" by "the beasts of the earth" may not be exactly the same in location. The regions affected by the devastating famines were extensive to cover the "fourth part of the earth" that Death and Hell had power over in killing "with hunger."

CHAPTER 4

THE FOURTH SEAL: KILL WITH SWORD

THE MONGOL EMPIRE

[Rev 6:8] And I looked, and behold a pale horse: and his name that sat on him was Death, and Hell followed with him. And power was given unto them over the fourth part of the earth, to kill with sword, and with hunger, and with death, and with the beasts of the earth.

Now it is time to examine the "sword" mentioned in the passage above. Examining "pestilence" and "famine" suggests that the Scripture chronologically listed the events within one seal.

As the study revealed, the Great European Famine (1315–1317) came before the Black Death in Europe (1348–1350). Therefore, the incident which kills with the sword should come prior to the Great European Famine. The initial research began by looking into incidents where a war was fought using the sword causing massacre before 1315 and 1350 which are periods of the Great European Famine and the Black Death.

WAR	PERIOD	DEATH TOLL
The Crusades	1095–1291	3,000,000
Albigensian Crusade	1208–1249	1,000,000
Hundred Years' War	1337–1453	3,000,000

Table 4-1. Major wars during the early second millennium including the Great European Famine and the Black Death period.[1]

The initial research did not reveal any war of particular significance during this period. Consequently, the search continued for other historic incidents prior to 1315.

But before examining the incidents leading up to 1315, there are things worth considering. The first noticeable characteristic of the descriptions of the fourth seal that distinguishes itself from other seals is how the descriptions for each event comprising the seal lack fine details.

For instance, the first seal writes about the rider of the white horse and further adds that the rider had a bow and a crown and went on conquering. The second seal which speaks about the red horse is also followed by detailed descriptions that the peace was taken from the earth, people killed one another, and was given a great sword. Likewise, the third seal also includes such detailed elements.

In contrast, the fourth seal only provides the rider's name and how he killed—"with sword." Of course, some may view the killing with sword, hunger, and pestilence (carried by beasts, as discussed in a previous chapter) as detailed description. However, these events of the sword, hunger, and pestilence do not seem to compose of a same simultaneous event, but separate and independent events. Moreover, these events must occur in history in the order of their sequential appearances in the Scripture; the killing with sword must come first before the hunger, and then the death by pestilence shall follow.

From this perspective, the description pertaining to the sword killing is rather brief. There is the name of Death given to the rider, the Hell followed with him, and to them was given the power over the fourth part of the earth. Among these, the part about the rider's name being Death and the Hell following with him already indicates a significant number of deaths to occur. Hence, the clue to this event—to kill with sword—other than hinting that it may involve a big warlike incident, does not provide any new information.

At any rate, without any additional extractable information, the passage has a very definite clue in and of itself—the power given over the fourth part of "planet Earth." This clue in turn serves as the telltale evidence signifying that this event is readily noticeable by its magnitude from historical perspectives. Scripture writes in succinct manner without superfluous details. Nonetheless, the given information is sufficient to define the seal as a unique incident in history.

Again, the fourth seal—sword, hunger (famine), and pestilence—had been brought to completion, one by one, demonstrated by history.

If so, here is a new question to answer: What is the big warlike incident that took many people's lives that was so obvious yet happened before 1315? Some readers may have already landed on the answer. This is no other than the war initiated by Genghis Khan, who left the legacy of world domination in world history.

It is probably unnecessary to provide detailed explanation of who Genghis Khan (c. 1162–1227) is since he is such a prominent figure in history. The Great Mongol Empire that he and his followers built was the largest contiguous empire in human history, covering the Eurasian Continent. The information on how he grew up, how he unified the numerous confederations, and how he conquered the world is easily accessible; therefore, it will not be discussed in this book.

The Scripture states that a quarter of planet Earth is affected by the fourth seal events. Furthermore, the names provided by the Scripture as Death and Hell indicate an enormous death toll to be the result of the fourth seal events. The previous chapters have established that the famines and pestilence have caused extremely high death tolls. Likewise, the death toll that resulted from Genghis Khan will also be examined in this chapter.

MASSACRE BY THE MONGOLS

Let us first examine how the Mongol invasion impacted China. The Mongol invasion in the thirteenth century is said to have reduced China's population by 35 million. Northern China was the most populated part of China back then, and only a quarter of its population survived the Mongol invasion. The population of the Jin dynasty was 50 million, according to the census in 1195. With the Mongol invasion, it drastically diminished to 8.5 million, and caused a major southward shift of population in China.[2]

ABC News once cited Matthew White's *The Great Big Book of Horrible Things: The Definitive Chronicle of History's 100 Worst Atrocities*, in which he lists the tragedy of approximately 40 million people having been killed by Genghis Khan's army between 1206 and 1227.[3]

The New York Times also referenced the same book to report that 11.1 percent of the world population had died from the

Mongol invasion.[4] This is to say, if the Mongol invasion were to have happened in 2016, with its estimated population of about 7.4 billion, a death toll of 11.1 percent would have equaled to loss of 820 million people.

In other words, analyzing the extent of the world's largest atrocities by the percentage of world's population reduction, the invasion of the Mongol Empire decisively ranks at the top. According to the number of deaths, it was during the World War II that the largest number of people lost lives, totaling 66 million. However, percentage-wise, this figure merely reaches 2.6 percent of world population at that time. Hence, ranking the death toll by the percentage of the world population reduction at the time would certainly have the Mongol invasion at the top.

POWER GIVEN OVER THE FOURTH PART OF THE EARTH

As discussed previously, the description in the fourth seal—the fourth part of the earth (τὸ τέταρτον τῆς γῆς, *to tetarton tēs gēs*)—possibly indicates one fourth of the surface area of planet Earth. And if the Mongol Invasion is indeed the kill-by-sword event of the fourth seal, then the Mongol Empire must have attempted to prevail over the entire conceivable world.

The Mongol Empire enjoyed its maximum territory under the reign of Genghis' grandson, Kublai Khan (1215–1294). Let's take note of the following excerpt about Kublai Khan:

On 23 September 1215, almost four months after Beijing fell, back in the Mongolian heartland, a royal child was born who, as khan of khans, the Great Khan, would accept the challenge of Genghis's impossible vision, and do more than any other leader to make it a reality. With an authority that reached, albeit shakily, from the Pacific to southern Russia, he would become the most powerful man who had ever lived – who *would* ever live until the emergence of the modern superpowers. He would hold nominal sway over one-fifth of the world's populated land masses, perhaps half of all humanity. His name would spread far beyond the areas he conquered, to Europe, to Japan, to Vietnam, to Indonesia: those sea-cucumber gatherers, harvesting their delicacies off northern Australia, would perhaps hear of his attempt to invade Java in 1292. It was the legend of his wealth that, two centuries after his death, would inspire Columbus to head westward on a voyage that ended, not in a new route to an ancient land, but in the chance rediscovery of one long forgotten. Had he not existed, had there been no Mongol empire in China, who, I wonder, would have rediscovered America?[5]

Then let us now find out how much of the land area the Mongol Empire occupied. As said before, the Empire begun with Genghis Khan had reached its peak size at the time of his grandson, Kublai Khan. This means that the size of the empire, marked by the conquered land, changed over time. Therefore, the reference time frame should be determined to properly assess the size of conquered land accordingly. The Scripture says that the rider on the horse of the fourth seal kills with the sword. Therefore, the investigation must concentrate on the coverage of the killing field by the sword.

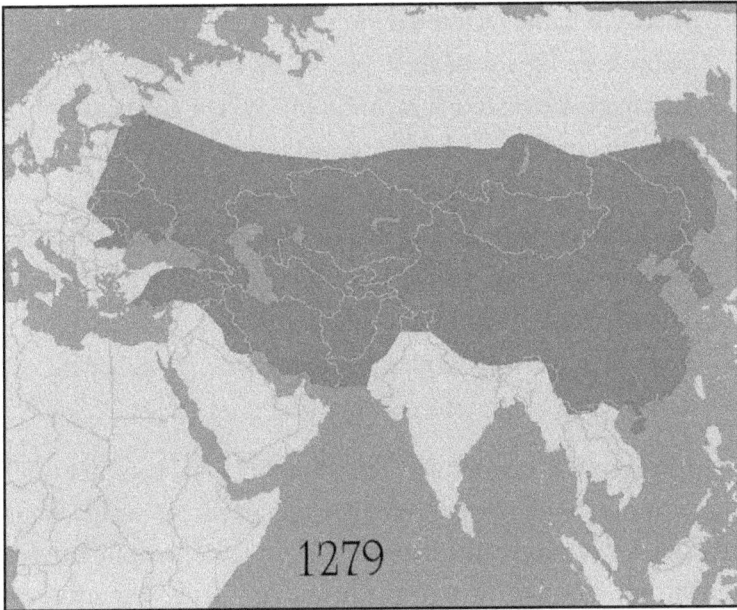

Fig. 4-1. Map of the Mongolian Empire in 1279 at the time of Kublai Khan.[6]

It is a common knowledge that the Mongols decimated the population as they conquered new areas. The Mongol generals gave opponents the opportunity to surrender. If they conceded to surrender, the opponents had to pay tribute or become contributing troops to Mongols. But with any resistance, the Mongols executed massive destruction and terror, leaving the resistant force devastated to the point of annihilation.

Here is an example from Kublai Khan's reign when a general under his charge, Ariq-khaya, attacked Fancheng near the city of Xiangyang in Song dynasty:

The city had to die, very publicly. In the Muslim campaigns, artisans, women and children had often been spared, because they could be enslaved. But there was no point keeping any of these people alive. No distinction was made between young and old, civilian and soldier, man, woman and child. Some 3,000 soldiers and an estimated 7,000 others had their throats cut like cattle, the bodies being piled up in a mound to make sure that the massacre was visible from Xiangyang. In Richard Davis's words, "Nothing could demoralize Xiangyang's defenders like this grotesque sight and the terrifying message it so forcefully conveyed."[7]

Carnage was common as the Mongols advanced. They left many mounds of piled skulls that remained for years. Some researchers even revealed that the carbon level had plummeted during the era due to too much killing.[8] Truly, the army of Mongols conquered the land with the sword, and with it debilitated the enemies with mass slaughter. The Mongol empire grew its size as they "kill with sword." Perhaps this provides enough reason that the point in time when the Mongol empire reached its maximum expansion should be the reference time frame to appropriately calculate the conquered land.

According to various sources, the largest Mongol Empire thrived at the Kublai Khan, circa 1279. The conquered area then amounted to about 12.7 million square miles or 33 million square kilometers.[9, 10, 11]

Now it is time to calculate how much of the Earth's land area 33 million square kilometers take up. In earlier chapter, the total habitable land area—the entire land area on Earth excluding Antarctica—was calculated to be 134,940,000 km². Therefore, the land area covered by Mongol Empire compared to the total habitable land on Earth is 33,000,000 km² /

$134{,}940{,}000 \text{ km}^2 = 0.245 = 24.5$ percent. This figure confirms the Scripture's description of the rider in the fourth seal having power over the fourth part, 25 percent, of Earth to kill with the sword.

Some may question how America can be included in the calculation of the land area. The indigenous people were living in the land of America at the time, thus the American continent is legitimately included as part of "planet Earth." Therefore, when God refers to the land of Earth, it is unlikely that God only referred to Europe and Asia. In line with the argument, the uninhabited Antarctica covered with ice was excluded from calculation.

Timothy Snyder, a professor at Yale University, responded to the question "What Day Most Changed the Course of History?" in this way:

> On December 11, 1241, the Mongol warrior Batu Khan was poised to take Vienna and destroy the Holy Roman Empire. No European force could have kept his armies from reaching the Atlantic. But the death of Ögedei Khan, the second Great Khan of the Mongol empire, forced Batu Khan to return to Mongolia to discuss the succession. Had Ögedei Khan died a few years later, European history as we know it would not have happened.[12]

The Mongol invasion certainly set the precedence for other massacres to follow in history. Although some argue that people evolve to nurture the goodness in human nature as opposed to the evil, the lessons of history prove that humans have repeated massacres in various forms in different times in history.

With regard to his book, *The Better Angels of Our Nature: Why Violence Has Declined*, Steven Pinker, professor of psychology at Harvard University, claimed: "I think there is also a non-negligible chance that within the next 25 to 50 years there will be fewer bloodthirsty despots, and that nuclear weapons could be abolished."[13] And again to a question, "Has human nature, specifically our inclination toward violence, changed? Or is it more a change in how this inclination manifests itself?" he answered that: "I argue for the latter, although it's not inconceivable that the former has taken place, that we have literally evolved so that the more pacific parts of human nature have been strengthened, at least over a span of centuries or millennia. I have a lengthy discussion in the book for how that could happen: it's certainly biologically possible."[14]

By contrast, the Bible says that the distressing time will come in the last days.

[2Ti 3:1] This know also, that in the last days perilous times shall come.

[2Ti 3:2] For men shall be lovers of their own selves, covetous, boasters, proud, blasphemers, disobedient to parents, unthankful, unholy,

[2Ti 3:3] Without natural affection, trucebreakers, false accusers, incontinent, fierce, despisers of those that are good,

[2Ti 3:4] Traitors, heady, highminded, lovers of pleasures more than lovers of God;

[2Ti 3:5] Having a form of godliness, but denying the power thereof: from such turn away.

This passage does not claim that people undergo changes due to the distressing environment in the last days. In contrast, the Bible clearly indicates that people will progressively become ungodly in the last days and such regression in intrinsic nature engenders perilous times. Moreover, the Scripture warns of a bloodthirsty despot Antichrist who will kill many in the last days.

THE RELATIONSHIP AMONG SWORD, FAMINE, AND PESTILENCE

The population of China in 1200, before the Mongol invasion, was around 123 million; whereas, by 1393 it declined to 65 million.[15] According to another source, China's population in 1250 was 112 million, but by 1500 it was barely 84 million.[16] This large reduction seems to be the result of the Mongol invasion, the famine, and the plague.

YEAR (AD)	WORLD POPULATION (MILLIONS)	
	LOWER	UPPER
1200	360	450
1250	400	416
1300	360	432
1340	443	N/A
1400	350	374

Table 4-2. Historical Estimates of World Population.[17]

As seen from Table 4-2 of the world population, both the lower estimate and the upper estimate from year 1200 to 1300 seem to suggest the population has not significantly increased during that time. This is the period during the

Mongol invasion, when Genghis Khan initiated the conquest in 1206 and continued to expand the empire. In the year 1279, the Song dynasty collapsed at the hands of Kublai Khan, and the Mongol Empire occupied its greatest territory.

As discussed before, the Black Death depopulated the world from 1340 to 1400. Overall, the world population from 1200 to 1400 decreased or remained stagnant. The phenomenon is attributed to the massacre performed by the Mongol army, the Great Famine, and the Black Death.

After the Mongol Invasion, a large region ranging from the Southeast Asia to the Eastern Europe was united under one political authority. The Eurasian unification by the Mongol Empire brought forth a historical exchange between Europe and Asia, the so-called Pax Mongolica. Under such administration of Mongol Empire, cultural exchange and collaboration in commerce began, which further brought stability of social, cultural, and economic life for the people under the reign. The Mongols utilized the skills and technologies from the conquered regions for their own advancement, and this eventually stimulated further exchange between the Eastern and Western cultures.[18]

Such exchanges were well-facilitated by the Silk Road. However, the Silk Road also provided a channel to spread the plague to Europe. It was 1338 when the Black Death first broke out, and it was caused by military encounter with the Mongols. Let us review a report on the abovementioned facts:

> . . . from the mid-thirteenth century, increased commercialization in Europe opened up silk routes through the steppe lands, and the trading posts set up to service this trade formed convenient stepping-stones for infected fleas to break out of the area.

The first known victims of plague were probably a community of Nestorian Christians at Issyk Kul, south of Lake Balkash, whose cemetery explicitly records three plague victims in 1338-9, a year in which there were unusually heavy mortalities. In 1343, it had reached the Black Sea port of Kaffa (Theodosia) in the Crimea.

There, a Genoese colony was under siege from a khan of the Golden Horde named Yannibeg, when his army was decimated by an outbreak of plague. Determined to make his enemies suffer the torments of his men, he ordered that bodies of plague victims be catapulted into the city. The Genoese hurriedly dumped these into the sea, but the plague spread anyway. Taking to their ships, the fleeing Genoese carried the plague far and wide.[19]

This clearly indicates that the spread of the Black Death and the Mongols' conquest are powerfully related. There is also a report evidencing the relationship between the spread of the Black Death and the famine:

Europe was then going through a cooling period known as the Little Ice Age, which reduced harvests and led to heavy rains that drowned out crops, in turn leading to famine and malnutrition. Economic downturns left large swaths of the population in poverty and squalor. The financial strains, the lack of public hygiene and sanitation, and an already weakened population made for ripe ground for a contagious and pathogenic bug like *Y. pestis* to flourish.[20]

At some point in time during the Mongol invasion, much of Chinese populace was killed or relocated as refugees, giving rise to economic impoverishment primarily because the farming and trading became disrupted. Inevitably, the widespread famine must have been the natural aftermath.

As revealed before, the Black Death has first started from China following the famine. But more interestingly, this plague has caused the Mongol Empire, or more specifically, Yuan Dynasty into decline.[21]

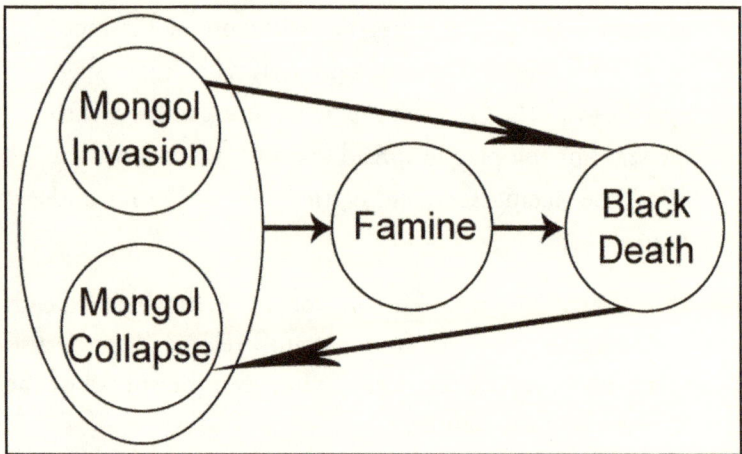

Fig. 4-2. The Relationship among the Mongol Empire, the Great Famine, and the Black Death.

Such facts indicate that the events of the fourth seal— the sword, famine, and pestilence—are all inter-related. God has mentioned all sword, famine, and pestilence within one category in the fourth seal. Could it be an indication that God intended us to know that these events are connected to one another?

Genghis Khan's conquest would not have been possible by his own power alone, but was with the help of climate change. Recently, scientists have analyzed the growth rings of Siberia pine trees in the central Mongolia that date back nearly 2,000 years. The result showed that between 1180 and 1190, which was right before Genghis Khan established his hegemony, there was a severe drought. The drought caused the power struggle that aided Genghis Khan in his rise to power through the political turbulence. Moreover, from 1211 to 1225 when Genghis Khan was on the conquest, there was ample precipitation and good weather. Such conditions made unusual plant productivity possible, which was ideal for grazing horses, directly translating to more horsepower. *The Independent* magazine once testified:

> The tree rings show that the normally cold, arid steppes of central Asia experienced their mildest, wettest weather in more than 1,000 years at the time when Genghis rose to power and established his enormous land empire with the help of his sons.[22]

Therefore, as affirmed by the historical records as well as the Scriptures, God is meticulously in control of even the climate and weather to precisely fulfill what He has spoken:

> [Jer 10:13] When he uttereth his voice, there is a multitude of waters in the heavens, and he causeth the vapours to ascend from the ends of the earth; he maketh lightnings with rain, and bringeth forth the wind out of his treasures.

CHAPTER 5

THE FIRST SEAL:
A BOW AND A CROWN

IS THE RIDER ON A WHITE HORSE JESUS CHRIST?

The Scripture pertaining to the first seal is as follows:

[Rev 6:1] And I saw when the Lamb opened one of the seals, and I heard, as it were the noise of thunder, one of the four beasts saying, Come and see.

[Rev 6:2] And I saw, and behold a white horse: and he that sat on him had a bow; and a crown was given unto him: and he went forth conquering, and to conquer.

After the first seal is opened, there is a white horse with a crowned man riding on it with a bow, trying to conquer.

The integrity of interpretation on this passage is contingent on correct identification of the rider on the white horse. Varied interpretations exist, but this book shall focus on two mainstream views: the first views this rider as Lord Jesus Christ, and the second as the false prophet. In order to test the legitimacy of the claims that the rider may be Christ, it is imperative to study how Jesus is described and characterized in Revelation.

> [Rev 1:13] And in the midst of the seven candlesticks one like unto the Son of man, clothed with a garment down to the foot, and girt about the paps with a golden girdle.

> [Rev 1:14] His head and his hairs were white like wool, as white as snow; and his eyes were as a flame of fire;

> [Rev 1:18] I am he that liveth, and was dead; and, behold, I am alive for evermore, Amen; and have the keys of hell and of death.

In this passage, the appellations "one like unto the Son of man" and "he that liveth, and was dead" confirm that it is indeed Jesus who spoke to John and the churches from Chapters 1 to 3.

> [Rev 5:5] And one of the elders saith unto me, Weep not: behold, the Lion of the tribe of Juda, the Root of David, hath prevailed to open the book, and to loose the seven seals thereof.

> [Rev 5:6] And I beheld, and, lo, in the midst of the throne and of the four beasts, and in the midst of the elders, stood a Lamb as it had been slain, having seven horns and seven eyes, which are the seven Spirits of God sent forth into all the earth.

The "the Root of David" and "Lamb" in the passage strictly bespeak Jesus.

[Rev 6:16] And said to the mountains and rocks, Fall on us, and hide us from the face of him that sitteth on the throne, and from the wrath of the Lamb:

In the above passage, Jesus does not make the scene but is addressed as "the Lamb." It is an undeniable reference to Jesus.

[Rev 14:1] And I looked, and, lo, a Lamb stood on the mount Sion, and with him an hundred forty and four thousand, having his Father's name written in their foreheads.

The "Lamb" standing on the mount Sion absolutely speaks of Jesus.

[Rev 14:14] And I looked, and behold a white cloud, and upon the cloud one sat like unto the Son of man, having on his head a golden crown, and in his hand a sharp sickle.

Some argue that the passage above delineates an angel, but on the contrary, the reference to the one "like unto the Son of man" shall be attributed to Christ.

[Rev 19:11] And I saw heaven opened, and behold a white horse; and he that sat upon him was called Faithful and True, and in righteousness he doth judge and make war.

[Rev 19:12] His eyes were as a flame of fire, and on his head were many crowns; and he had a name written, that no man knew, but he himself.

[Rev 19:13] And he was clothed with a vesture dipped in blood: and his name is called The Word of God.

This passage in particular also makes it evident that the rider of a white horse is Jesus Christ, because it expounded his name: "The Word of God."

To draw a comprehensive conclusion, Revelation points to Jesus with words that serve as indisputably clear references such as "the Lamb," "the Son of man," or "the Word of God."

[Rev 7:2] And I saw another angel ascending from the east, having the seal of the living God: and he cried with a loud voice to the four angels, to whom it was given to hurt the earth and the sea,

Some propose that "another angel" from this passage is Jesus. However, Revelation always depicts Jesus with unequivocal clues in referencing Him. Therefore, "another angel" cannot be the Lord Jesus. Moreover, in all the referenced passages of Revelation, Jesus was never cited as an angel.

[Rev 10:1] And I saw another mighty angel come down from heaven, clothed with a cloud: and a rainbow was upon his head, and his face was as it were the sun, and his feet as pillars of fire:

In this example also, "another mighty angel" above cannot be God or Jesus Christ; another angel is simply another angel and not the Lord.

Here is what Robertson's *Word Pictures* has to say about the subject matter on the identity of the rider in Revelation 6:2:

Commentators have been busy identifying the rider of the white horse according to their various theories. "It is tempting to identify him with the Rider on the white horse in Rev 19:11, whose name is 'the Word of God'" (Swete). Tempting, "but the two riders have nothing in common beyond the white horse."[1]

As such, the rider on a white horse who was crowned cannot be asserted as Jesus with lacking evidence.

Then, why was a crown given to the rider? There are two kinds of crowns that appear in the Bible: one is a diadem (διάδημα, *diadēma*) primarily worn by kings, and the other is wreath (στέφανος, *stephanos*) usually given to the winner in a public game.[2]

The verse below shows that even Satan wears such crowns:

[Rev 12:3] And there appeared another wonder in heaven; and behold a great red dragon, having seven heads and ten horns, and seven crowns (διάδημα, *diadēma*) upon his heads.

The very crowns Satan wears are the diadem kind as he is "prince of this world" (Jn 16:11). Not surprisingly, the Antichrist also has crowns, and they are also the diadem (διάδημα, *diadēma*) kind. This point is shown in the following verse:

[Rev 13:1] And I stood upon the sand of the sea, and saw a beast rise up out of the sea, having seven heads and ten horns, and upon his horns ten crowns (διάδημα, *diadēma*), and upon his heads the name of blasphemy.

Assuredly, Jesus also had diadems (διάδημα, *diadēma*) on His head:

[Rev 19:12] His eyes were as a flame of fire, and on his head were many crowns (διάδημα, *diadēma*); and he had a name written, that no man knew, but he himself.

[Rev 19:13] And he was clothed with a vesture dipped in blood: and his name is called The Word of God.

Now, it is time to compare the rider on a white horse of the first seal to Lord Jesus:

[Rev 6:2] And I saw, and behold a white horse: and he that sat on him had a bow; and a crown (στέφανος, *stephanos*) was given unto him: and he went forth conquering, and to conquer.

[Rev 14:14] And I looked, and behold a white cloud, and upon the cloud one sat like unto the Son of man, having on his head a golden crown (στέφανος, *stephanos*), and in his hand a sharp sickle.

As established previously, the figure in Revelation chapter 14 is Jesus Christ. Yet, Jesus here is not wearing the diadem (διάδημα, *diadēma*) but a wreath (στέφανος, *stephanos*), a symbol for victory. And likewise, the rider on a white horse in Revelation chapter 6 is also wearing a winner's wreath (στέφανος, *stephanos*).

However, in contrast, Jesus is wearing the "golden" wreath, whereas the rider on a white horse from the first seal is wearing a mere wreath. The diadem (διάδημα, *diadēma*) worn by kings symbolizes authority, and therefore, requires no further ornate description like "golden diadem." However, wreaths (στέφανος, *stephanos*) are usually made of some metallic substance or even plants. Therefore, Jesus' "golden"wreath can truly be distinguished from a regular wreath. The symbolic difference here demonstrates that the rider in the first seal is inferior to Jesus, and that he is not a true victor.

So far, the investigations have established that the descriptions of Jesus in Revelation accompany clearly identifiable expressions of who He is. The crown that He wore was the victor's "golden" wreath (στέφανος, *stephanos*) and many diadems (διάδημα, *diadēma*) that Kings wear.

In sum, Jesus has many diadems (διάδημα, *diadēma*) on His head (singular); Satan has seven diadems (διάδημα, *diadēma*) on seven heads; the Antichrist has ten diadems (διάδημα, *diadēma*) on ten horns.

The next question to probe is whether John's description of the rider befits the characteristics of Jesus.

[Rev 1:19] Write the things which thou hast seen, and the things which are, and the things which shall be hereafter;

John wrote in Revelation of the things "which (he) had seen," the things "which are," and the things "which shall be hereafter." The first two categories are what John had seen of Jesus' appearance, the seven stars and the seven golden candlesticks in chapter 1, and the status of seven churches then in Asia Minor in chapters 2 and 3. The last category of "which shall be hereafter" falls in chapters 6 through 22. This is based on the conventionally accepted interpretation.

However, the Scriptures from Revelation chapters 6 to 22 are prophecies shown to John, events that are to happen after John. Therefore, Revelation chapter 6 is not describing Jesus, because the first seal occurs later than John's time, but way before the return of Jesus Christ which is prophesied in Revelation chapter 19. Jesus does not return until the final war. Furthermore, John would never describe the Messiah as someone trying to go forth to conquer. Indeed, Jesus will unilaterally achieve victory in the final war, but that war is not about conquering and to conquer.

The verse regarding the first seal illustrates the rider's strong will to conquer something, which is quite contrary to the image of the Lord, who had already gained the ultimate victory. Jesus does not need to try to conquer, as He had already triumphed over all on the cross (Col 2:15).

> [Rev 6:2] And I saw, and behold a white horse: and he that sat on him had a bow; and a crown was given unto him: and he went forth conquering, and to conquer.

Another point to address is the possession of a bow, yet missing arrows. Deriving from this fact, perhaps the rider does not (or cannot) hurt directly with sharp-edged objects, but may victimize souls through manipulations and scheming. Dearth of de facto description of his weapon signifies it does not typify a secular regime with armaments.

Some champion the interpretation that the rider refers to personified Rome or Roman military power, but it is highly unlikely as explained above. Rather than the political force, the rider here must be a false prophet in the embodiment of a religious entity.

Judging from the fact that the rider with a bow also had a wreath (στέφανος, *stephanos*), the passage suggests the rider is successful and victorious in seducing the souls through his schemes. Regarding this, the Lord had forewarned about such deceivers:

[Mt 24:5] For many shall come in my name, saying, I am Christ; and shall deceive many.

Then, who is this rider and what kind of established order does it represent? What must be addressed is the fact that the false prophet or the deceiving system had been given the winner's wreath by a separate external entity. Since the white horse in question is symbolic, the rider also could be symbolic. By the same token, the rider can symbolize the false prophet himself or some sort of a system, organization, or an order that the false prophet established on earth.

But the notion that "a crown was given unto him" in Revelation 6:2 can be looked at as a specific incident on earth. It could refer to a defining moment when the false prophet's system is firmly propped up in place. This view is strengthened by the Scriptures since the rider "went forth conquering, and to conquer" to build his power and empire, after receiving the wreath.

This begs the quest for identifying the exact incident of the first seal in history. This must have occurred posterior to the end of the first century when Revelation was written, but prior to the year 1206 when Genghis Khan of the fourth seal emerged. The incident of the first seal, therefore, is highly related to the early church history. The rise of the false prophet must have the pseudo form of Christianity, showing great similarity to Christianity while fundamentally different. This characteristic is found in the Papal system.

CONSTANTINE THE GREAT

Before examining the establishment of the papacy, understanding the spread of Christianity through the Roman Empire can help interpret the first seal.

Despite much persecution arising from the conflicts with pagan state religion, Christianity during the first century spread throughout the Roman Empire. Such wide-spread expansion of Christianity was founded on the bloodshed of many martyrs. Persecution was truly excruciating, but bore much fruit. By the time this persecution was over, Christianity prevailed in entire Roman Empire. The persecution began in the year 64 with Emperor Nero and lasted until 313, when Emperor Constantine I (Constantine the Great, 272–337) reigned.[3]

In 313, Constantine the Great, who ruled the west, and Emperor Licinius, who reigned over Balkans in the east, met for political reasons and proclaimed *the Edict of Milan*. *The Edict of Milan* warranted absolute religious freedom for Christians; therefore, it put an end to period of persecution against Christians and established a fresh foundation for Christendom. The following excerpt is from the beginning and the end portions of *the Edict of Milan*:

When we, Constantine and Licinius, emperors, had an interview at Milan, and conferred together with respect to the good and security of the commonweal, it seemed to us that, amongst those things that are profitable to mankind in general, the reverence paid to the Divinity merited our first and chief attention, and that it was proper that the Christians and all others should have liberty to follow that mode of religion which to each of them appeared best; so that that God, who is seated in heaven, might be benign and propitious to us, and to every one under our government . . . the open and free exercise of their respective religions is granted to all others, as well as to the Christians. For it befits the well-ordered state and the tranquillity of our times that each individual be allowed, according to his own choice, to worship the Divinity; and we mean not to derogate aught from the honour due to any religion or its votaries.[4]

Constantine the Great utilized churches as tools for Roman Empire to earn God's favor. But soon after he declared religious liberty for Christians, he was confronted with which sects of Christianity to support, and this enigma required discernment about which sect is of the true creed.[5]

So Roman Emperor Constantine I convened the First Council of Nicaea in 325 where the relationship between the Son of God and God the Father was theologically defined. Applying the formula of Trinity, the Council denounced any sect with a differing doctrine, and formally damned other beliefs as heretic, particularly Arianism. The following is the excerpt from the *Nicene Creed:*

We believe in one God, the Father Almighty, maker of all things visible and invisible; and in one Lord Jesus Christ, the Son of God, the only-begotten of his Father, of the substance of the Father, God of God, Light of Light, very God of very God, begotten, not made, being of one substance with the Father. By whom all things were made, both which be in heaven and in earth. Who for us men and for our salvation came down [from heaven] and was incarnate and was made man. He suffered and the third day he rose again, and ascended into heaven. And he shall come again to judge both the quick and the dead. And [we believe] in the Holy Ghost. And whosoever shall say that there was a time when the Son of God was not, or that before he was begotten he was not, or that he was made of things that were not, or that he is of a different substance or essence [from the Father] or that he is a creature, or subject to change or conversion— all that so say, the Catholic and Apostolic Church anathematizes them.[6]

The bishops of great cities of the Empire at the time were inevitably considered preeminent compared to the bishops of other regions. For this reason, the office of the archbishop, or metropolitan, came into existence. The rights of the archbishops are mentioned for the first time in the sixth canon of the Council of Nicaea:

The old custom in Egypt, Libya, and the Pentapolis shall continue to be observed, so that the bishop of Alexandria shall exercise authority over all these regions, for the bishop of Rome enjoys a similar right. Similarly in Antioch and in the other provinces the churches shall retain their prerogatives. Moreover let it be known that should any one have become bishop without the approval of the metropolitan, this great council has ordained that such an one shall not be regarded as a bishop.[7]

When Constantine the Great convened the religious Council of Nicaea, he was initially welcomed by all the denominations of Christians to serve as an arbitrator on religious matters. However, Constantine I gradually came to think of himself as a "'bishop among bishops,' even a presiding imperial bishop who could himself offer a suggestion as to the orthodox theological formula for the relation of the Son of God to the Father."[8]

As Constantine I wanted to assume his role as both the king and priest to control every facet of the Empire, with passage of time, some theopolitical parties found the Emperor's favor while others were outcast. The disfavored sects regressed to a position in libeling the Emperor as a heretic and even labeling him the predecessor of the Antichrist.[9]

Consequently, the idea to separate church and state resurfaced as Bishop Ambrose of Milan voiced that the Emperor must keep out of religious matters, as things that belong to Caesar and God are distinct. Such philosophy soon transformed into superiority of church over state, and this made friction between the emperors and the bishops.[10]

THEODOSIUS THE GREAT

The last Roman Emperor to rule both the Latin West and the Byzantine Empire in the East was Emperor Theodosius I (Theodosius the Great, 347–395). Though it was by Constantine the Great that Christianity gained religious freedom, it was not until several decades later that Christianity became the official religion of the Roman Empire, as decreed in *the Theodosian Code* by Emperor Theodosius I in 380.

What makes *the Theodosian Code* special is that it banned all other non-Christian religions by declaring them illegal, forcing all to become Christians—not a mere Christian but specifically a "Catholic Christian" who adopts the holy Trinity. The relevant section of *the Theodosian Code* is as follows:

> It is our desire that all the various nation which are subject to our clemency and moderation, should continue to the profession of that religion which was delivered to the Romans by the divine Apostle Peter, as it has been preserved by faithful tradition and which is now professed by the Pontiff Damasus and by Peter, Bishop of Alexandria, a man of apostolic holiness. According to the apostolic teaching and the doctrine of the Gospel, let us believe in the one deity of the father, Son and Holy Spirit, in equal majesty and in a holy Trinity. We authorize the followers of this law to assume the title Catholic Christians; but as for the others, since in our judgment they are foolish madmen, we decree that they shall be branded with the ignominious name of heretics, and shall not presume to give their conventicles the name of churches.[11]

Christianity underwent colossal changes following the time of Emperor Constantine I, when religious liberty was granted. Prior to then, believing in the Lord entailed enduring persecution and putting one's life at stake in worst cases.

After Christianity became the official religion, being a Christian no longer subjected one to any persecution, but, on the contrary, even ushered in prerogatives and variety of social privileges. This especially became more so after Emperor Theodosius I's edict to outlaw all other religions except Christianity. As a consequence, Christianity on the outside flourished in numbers of believers, but also consolidated the authoritative power in the clergy class.

POPE LEO I

Among the popes of the Western Roman Empire, the pope that played a vital role in establishing the papacy was Pope Leo I (c. 400–461). He is the first pope to have the title, "the Great," appended to his name. Despite the burdens of the declining West and the controversial dogmas in the church, Pope Leo faced the challenges with sagacity to strengthen the church.[12]

In 452 when Attila the Hun sacked northern Italy, Leo courageously negotiated with Attila as an emperor's envoy to motivate his retreat from Italy. Also in 455 during Vandal Genseric's invasion, Leo persuaded the barbarians from completely burning the city of Rome and to spare people's lives. Although he could not prevent Rome from being captured, his intercession was greatly appreciated by the people.[13]

Three years after the Pope Leo I encountered Attila to salvage Rome, Prosper, a Christian chronicler, wrote about the incident of 452:

> Now Attila, having once more collected his forces which had been scattered in Gaul, took his way through Pannonia into Italy . . . To the emperor and the senate and Roman people none of all the proposed plans to oppose the enemy seemed so practicable as to send legates to the most savage king and beg for peace. Our most blessed Pope Leo – trusting in the help of God, who never fails the righteous in their trials – undertook the task, accompanied by Avienus, a man of consular rank, and the perfect Trygetius. And the outcome was what

his faith had foreseen; for when the king had received the embassy, he was so impressed by the presence of the high priest that he ordered his army to give up warfare and, after he had promised peace, he departed beyond the Danube.[14]

Contemporary historians' assessment of Leo is also that of a great leader. Bronwen writes of Leo's characteristics: "deep pastoral concern for the spiritual welfare of his congregation in Rome and with unity and order within all the churches of the Christian East and West, matched by a practical concern for the material needs of the civic community and its protection from invaders."[15]

HOW THE BISHOP OF ROME ROSE TO POWER

With the disintegration of Western Roman Empire in 476, the church broke from the state and gradually ruled over both religious and secular matters. But it was only after a course of momentous incidents that the Bishop of Rome established sole standing authority.

In early church days, the bishops of Rome did not enjoy any power. It was not until the Constantine the Great converted to Christianity that freedom of religion was even possible. Christianity was no longer a persecuted religion but rather the Empire's preferred official religion.

In 330, Constantine I transferred the capital from Rome to Constantinople (current Istanbul). The transference of capital to the eastern section of the Roman Empire practically divided the Empire into western and eastern halves. As he occupied the newly founded eastern portion, the Eastern Roman Empire eventually acquired a new name, "Byzantine Empire," and the

Lateran Palace was given to the Bishop of Rome in the West. Although unsure about the exact date, scholars speculate it to be prior to 311 during the pontificate of Pope Miltiades, after which the ancient palace became the primary papal residence and the cathedral of Rome.[16]

Rome had many advantages to becoming the center of the papal powers. Two of the most important factors are, first, being the largest city in the Western Empire, and secondly, Rome being the only metropolitan church in the West, compared to four existing in the East.[17]

As Catholics uphold Peter as the first instituted pope and the founder—the rock upon which Jesus said to build the church (Mt 16:18–19)—of the Roman church, Rome lavished in tremendous prestige by claiming possession of the "keys of the kingdom of heaven" given to Peter.[18]

In contrast to Rome, Alexandria and Antioch in the East were downplayed as mere two of five chief churches, and the rivalry became quite fierce after Constantinople became the new capital.[19]

But to no avail, the Bishop of Rome continued to retain its privilege as a head of the five metropolitan churches—Constantinople, Alexandria, Antioch, Jerusalem, and Rome, where Rome being the only one in the West. As the head of church, the Pope of Rome enjoyed great authority. But due to the threats from foreign invasion and barbarian tribes, their power was practically limited.[20]

For strategic reasons, the capital of Western Roman Empire had moved to Ravenna in 402. Although Rome was no longer the official capital, it was still a city with rich legacies and spiritual authorities. For this reason, King Alaric, also known as King of the Visigoths, sacked Rome in 410. This resulted in the successful siege of Rome that had not happened in about eight hundred years. The fall of Rome greatly surprised not only the Romans but also their enemies. Thus, the words of St. Jerome adequately captured the Visigothic sack of Rome: "The City which had taken the whole world was itself taken."[21]

CLOVIS I

After Rome had fallen to the Goths, there was another historic incident that overturned the situation for the better of Catholicism. Through the conversion of pagan king Clovis I (c. 466–c. 511) of the Franks to the Catholic faith, Catholicism, which was antagonistic to Arianism, not only became dominant, but also gained military strength. With the augmented power in religion, politics, and military, now the Catholics could defend, expand, and influence the future.

The pagan Clovis I the Great, king of the Franks in Northern Gaul, acquired sovereignty over much of the northern and central parts of Roman Gaul. He conquered the last enclave of the Roman rule in Gaul, and united the Frankish tribes in the region of the already fallen Western Roman Empire. He is considered to be the founder of the Merovingian dynasty.[22]

Clovis I converted to Catholicism and was baptized in 496. As said before, Arianism was already declared heretic in 325 at the First Council of Nicaea, but the majority of Christian Gaul then were Gothic Arians while Catholics were minority. The conversion of Clovis I to Catholicism and not to Arianism, therefore, is quite significant, since his conquests expanded to nearly all Gaul, influencing western and central Europe.

This is how Clovis I came to receive baptism. Clovis' wife, Clotilde, was a Christian. Clotilde pleaded with her husband to convert, but he woud not accede to her request. Although she succeeded in having her son, Ingomer, baptized, he died soon afterwards. Their son's death made Clovis reproach Clotilde bitterly. Another son was born whom Clotilde made receive baptism. The son fell ill after baptism, but did not die.[23]

Thereafter, a war broke out with the Alemanni, and a Columbia University professor, James Harvey Robinson, writes about Clovis' episode during the war:

> It happened that the two armies were in battle, and there was great slaughter. Clovis' army was near to utter destruction. He saw the danger; his heart was stirred; he was moved to tears, and he raised his eyes to heaven, saying: "Jesus Christ, whom Clotilde declares to be the son of the living God, who it is said givest aid to the oppressed, and victory to those who put their hope in thee, I beseech the glory of thy aid. If thou shalt grant me victory over these enemies and I test that power which people consecrated to thy name say they have proved concerning thee, I will believe in thee and be baptized in thy name. For I have called upon my gods, but, as I have proved, they are far removed from my aid. So I believe that they have no power, for they do not succor those who serve them. Now I call upon thee, and I long to believe in thee – all the more that I may escape my enemies." When he had said these things, the Alemanni turned their backs and began to flee. When they saw that their king was killed, they submitted to the sway of Clovis, saying: "We wish that no more people should perish. Now we are thine." When the king had forbidden further war and praised his soldiers, he told

the queen how he had won the victory by calling on the name of Christ.[24]

Clovis received baptism and so did three thousand or more soldiers following him.[25] Clovis' conversion not only endowed the Catholic Church with political endorsement, but also with military power to sway the future of Europe. Therefore, the alliance between the pope and Clovis was "destined to have a great influence upon the history of Western Europe."[26]

In 507, the Visigoth line of defense was broken by Clovis. By cutting their military supply line, Clovis recovered southern Europe from the hands of Visigoths by 508. This achievement won Clovis the title of Roman Patricius and Consul from the Byzantine Emperor Anastasius[27] and also Clovis' succeeding kings of France the style "the Oldest Son of the Church" from the popes.[28] The recognition shows how significant was Clovis' contribution to laying the foundation for the first Catholic kingdom in the West.

Confirm the historic significance of this incident through couple of writers' remarks:

It is evident, from the language of Gregory of Tours, that this conflict between the Franks and the Visigoths was regarded by the orthodox party of his own and preceding ages as a religious war, on which, humanly speaking, the prevalence of the Catholic or the Arian creed in Western Europe depended.[29]

Nor was his a temporary conquest. The kingdom of the West Goths and the Burgundians had become the kingdom of the Franks. The invaders had at length arrived, who were to remain. It was decided that the Franks, and not the Goths, were to direct the future destinies of Gaul and Germany, and that the Catholic faith, and not Arianism, was to be the religion of these great realms.[30]

Now, the question is whether Clovis' triumph against the Visigoths in 508 is related to the Revelation's first seal event. If this is so, the wreath Clovis received would be the title of Roman Patricius and Consul, and the crown bestower would be Anastasius, the Byzantine emperor of the East.

However, such interpretation seems erroneous compared to the descriptions in the Scripture:

[Rev 6:2] And I saw, and behold a white horse: and he that sat on him had a bow; and a crown was given unto him: and he went forth conquering, and to conquer.

Since the crown (wreath) in the Scripture represents victory, it must be given as a sign of approval, recognition, or reward to a person for coming out triumphant in a competition. In this case, Clovis was found a victor in a battle against the Visigoths.

However, the problem is that the rider had a bow but "no arrows." In other words, the rider here cannot be a general or an emperor who actually fights in the war. Thus, the conquests achieved by Clovis cannot be interpreted as the Revelation's first seal, because Clovis fought with actual weapons.

In conclusion, the only qualifying historical incident would be the one where a crown was given to a horse rider, but the crown receiver should be a champion of a non-warrior origin.

JUSTINIAN THE GREAT

In interpreting the Revelation's first seal, the last person to review historically is an emperor of Byzantine Empire Justinian I (Justinian the Great, c. 482–565). During his reign, he tried to restore the empire to its former glory and conquered part of the lost territories in the west from the heretic barbarians.

When Justinian came to throne in 527, he engaged in raids against heretical barbarians and Persia that threatened the safety of Rome. In 533, with the help of General Belisarius, Justinian dispatched a fleet of five hundred ships to North Africa and conquered Vandal Kingdom in 534,[31] in order to deliver Africa from the Arian Vandal power that oppressed Catholics.[32] In 535, Belisarius sailed for Sicily to conquer the island, which he accomplished at once, and entered Rome in 536 and sustained a siege until the Goths retreated in 538.[33]

Thus, Rome was once again clear from the power of Ostrogoths, who believed in Arianism, and reoccupied by Catholic faith. Freed from Arian influence, the pope was now the undisputed head of the Catholic Church.[34]

THE JUSTINIAN CODE

Between 528 and 565, Justinian I compiled and reorganized then-existing Roman laws into a unified imperial code called *Corpus Juris Civilis*, also known as *the Justinian Code*.[35, 36] His legacy still serves as the basis for modern systems of civil law.

In the year 528, the first religious *edict of Justinian* was issued. There, the emperor declared unto all men that he adheres to the tradition and confession of the holy Catholic Church. It also pronounces an anathema, or curse, against all heretics, such as Nestorians, Eutychians, and Apollinarians.[37]

In one of the letters to Pope John II, Justinian styled the pope "head of all the Holy Churches":

Emperor Justinian, Victorious, Pious, Happy, Renowned, Triumphant, always Augustus, to John, Patriarch, and most Holy Archbishop of the fair City of Rome:

With honor to the Apostolic See, and to your Holiness, which is, and always has been remembered in Our prayers, both now and formerly, and honoring your happiness, as is proper in the case of one who is considered as a father, We hasten to bring to the knowledge of Your Holiness everything relating to the condition of the Church, as We have always had the greatest desire to preserve the unity of your Apostolic See, and the condition of the Holy Churches of God, as they exist at the present time, that they may remain without disturbance or opposition. Therefore, We have exerted Ourselves to unite all the priests of the East and subject them to the See of Your Holiness, and hence the questions which have at present arisen, although they are manifest and free from doubt, and according to the doctrines of your Apostolic See, are constantly firmly observed and preached by all priests, We have still considered it necessary that they should be brought to the attention of Your Holiness. For we do not suffer anything which has reference to the state of the Church, even though what causes difficulty may be clear and free from doubt, to be discussed without being brought to the notice of Your Holiness, because you are the head of all the Holy Churches, for We shall exert Ourselves in every way (as has already been stated), to increase the honor and authority of your See.[38]

Speculations date the letter to March 25, 533 or before, because Justinian writes on that date to Epiphanius that he had already dispatched the letter and repeats his decision: "all affairs touching the Church shall be referred to the Pope, Head of all Bishops, and the true and effective correcter of heretics."[39]

By and large, Justinian magnified the pope above all denominations by referring as "head of all the Holy Churches" and "corrector of heretics." In response, the pope wrote back Byzantine Emperor in 534:

John, Bishop of the City of Rome, to his most Illustrious and Merciful Son Justinian.

Among the conspicuous reasons for praising your wisdom and gentleness, Most Christian of Emperors, and one which radiates light as a star, is the fact that through love of the Faith, and actuated by zeal for charity, you, learned in ecclesiastical discipline, have preserved reverence for the See of Rome, and have subjected all things to its authority, and have given it unity. The following precept was communicated to its founder, that is to say, the first of the Apostles, by the mouth of the Lord, namely: "Feed my lambs."

This See is indeed the head of all churches, as the rules of the Fathers and the decrees of the Emperors assert, and the words of your most reverend piety testify. It is therefore claimed that what the Scriptures state, namely, "By Me Kings reign, and the Powers dispense justice;" will be accomplished in you. For there is nothing which shines with a more brilliant lustre than genuine faith when displayed by a prince, since there is nothing which prevents destruction as true religion does, for as both of them have reference to the Author of Life and Light, they disperse darkness and prevent apostasy. Wherefore, Most Glorious of Princes, the Divine Power is implored by the prayers of all to preserve your piety in this ardor for the Faith, in this devotion of your mind, and in this zeal for true religion, without failure, during your entire existence. For we believe that this is for the benefit of the Holy Churches, as it was written, "The king rules with his lips," and again, "The heart of the King is in the hand of God, and it will incline to whatever side God wishes"; that is to say, that He may confirm your empire, and maintain your kingdoms for the peace of the Church and the unity of religion; guard their authority, and preserve him in that sublime tranquility which is so grateful to him; and no small change is granted by the Divine Power through whose agency a divided church is not afflicted by any griefs or subject to any reproaches. For it is written, "A just king, who is upon his throne, has no reason to apprehend any misfortune."

We have received with all due respect the evidences of your serenity, through Hypatius and Demetrius, most holy men, my brothers and fellow-bishops, from whose statements we have learned that you have promulgated an Edict addressed to your faithful people, and dictated by your love of the Faith, for the purpose of overthrowing the designs of heretics, which is in accordance with the evangelical tenets, and which we have confirmed by our authority with the consent of our brethren and fellow bishops, for the reason that it is in conformity with the apostolic doctrine . . .[40]

Both letters to and from the pope were incorporated into *the Justinian Code* in 534, which not only authenticated the exchange of these letters having taken place, but also canonized the papal authority.[41]

In 545, *Novella 131* was issued and in Chapter II, it was declared that the Apostolic See of Rome was superior to the Archbishop of Constantinople in rank:

Concerning The Precedence of Patriarchs.

Hence, in accordance with the provisions of these Councils, We order that the Most Holy Pope of ancient Rome shall hold the first rank of all the Pontiffs, but the Most Blessed Archbishop of Constantinople, or New Rome, shall occupy the second place after the Holy Apostolic See of ancient Rome, which shall take precedence over all other sees.[42]

INTERPRETATION OF THE FIRST SEAL

The history hitherto presented requires further analysis to identify who or what force might have been depicted by the Revelation's rider of the white horse and the giver of the crown to the rider.

Unquestionably, it was God, the Author of history, who allowed the conferring of the crown.

[Ro 13:1] Let every soul be subject unto the higher powers. For there is no power but of God: the powers that be are ordained of God.

At any rate, the task here is to identify who was utilized as the agent of the crown giver. Again, identifying the time of crowning of the rider of the horse can validate the accuracy of the interpretation.

To repeat again, the crowned rider cannot be an emperor or a general, for he has no weapons. An entity that seduces souls of men such as false prophet can be considered, however. The rider's crown also suggests that he emerged triumphant from certain rivalry.

From the papal history visited, the Pope of Rome had risen above all bishops of metropolitan churches as the ultimate authoritative figure. His victory as the highest supremacy among bishops is acknowledged and solidified by emperor Justinian in *the Justinian Code*. And if the victory is symbolized by receiving the crown, what crown was given pope? It must be Justinian's appellation of pope as the "head of all the Holy Churches."

By reasoning, the crown-giver cannot be subordinate to the crown-receiver. In like manner, if Justinian is the crown-giver, his power shall exceed that of the Bishop of the City of Rome. And a historic incident elucidates the power structure of Justinian's time.

Although Justinian exalted the Bishop of Rome to the "head of all the Holy Churches" in 533, Justinian in reality put the bishop under his control. Such chain of commandment is evident from an incident where Justinian's general, Belisarius, deposed the Pope Silverius and sent him into exile in 537.[43]

Succeeding Silverius was Pope Vigilius, who was forced to embark on a ship to Constantinople, where he was practically treated as a prisoner for eight years as ordered by Justinian for not siding with him on a religious issue (in the matter of Three Chapters).[44] Therefore, judging by the fact that Justinian subordinated popes at will, his imperial sovereignty indisputably surpassed that of the popes.

Then, when was the time of crowning? Could it be 533 when Justinian wrote a letter addressing pope as the "head of all the Holy Churches," or is it 534 when *the Justinian Code* was declared? Or could it be 536, when Justinian's general, Belisarius, entered Rome to fight Ostrogoths, or is it 538 when Rome was entirely recaptured?

The exact date of crown bestowment is not so important. Rather, the focus shall be on the facts that the crown receiver was not the emperor or the general that actually fought in battles and that the time of crowning differed from the time of holding de facto power.

Yet, the crown represents stature and must be a public and official incident. In this regard, the year 534 when *Justinian's edict* publicly declared pope as the "head of all the Holy Churches" is the most likely time corresponding to the crowning incident.

The year 536, when Belisarius made his way through enemy lines to Rome, or the year 538, when Rome was totally taken back from Goths, may be contested as possible candidates of the crowning moment. However, these histories unfolded after the papal authority had been legally established in 534 and should rather be considered as incidents that aided in advancing the papal supremacy. Anyhow, judging from the successive years of power struggle between the papacy and the emperors, the retaking of Rome should not be regarded with significance.

What is significant is that the crown receiver goes forth conquering and to conquer, eventually outmatching the power of the original crown giver. Indeed, the rider of the horse should be identified as not only an actual individual, but also as a symbolic figure representing a systematic entity, because a white horse is a symbol to begin with. Thus, the receiving of a wreath shall be interpreted as the establishment of papal supremacy through a particular incident, and the rider as the papal system.

To this date, many have interpreted the Revelation's first seal as the rising of the Antichrist or the False Prophet, and consequently there has been a tendency to focus the first seal on the year 538. Also, many have interpreted 1,260 days of persecution in Revelation 12:6 as 1,260 years that will take for the papal system, or Antichrist's system, to fall. Adding 1,260 years (instead of days) to the year 538 renders 1798, about which date the *Encyclopedia Britannica* writes: "In 1798 General Berthier made his French army enter into Rome and took the pope captive, where he later died. And the papal government is abolished, and a secular one is set up."[45]

Such plausible, yet specious, interpretation is possible only if 1,260 days are replaced by 1,260 years and also if year 538 was when the papal power was instituted. Only then can the Bishop of Rome (the False Prophet) hold power to rule over 1,260 years (days) as prophesied in the Scriptures. Such interpretation was especially popular amongst the Adventists. However, 1,260 days must be kept as 3.5 years as Scripture records, as opposed to 1,260 years.

Verily, there may be dual interpretations possible for a particular prophecy. But even with the duality, it is by principle that the prophecy must first be interpreted by the letter, a day for a day. Based on this interpretational approach, associating the first seal with year 538 is farfetched. Instead, it is more credible to view the first seal as the incident in 534 when papal supremacy is codified into law.

The pervading papal influence today as the false prophet in Christianity and beyond is exemplified in the "Bayith Ministry chart" (Fig. 5-1). About the purpose and the approach to identifying the referenced names and organizations, the creator of the chart explains:

> ... every single name displayed here is directly connected with Romanists (This is with the possible exception of V. P. Wierwille, who nevertheless taught a variety of Babylonian doctrines). Roman Catholics idolize: Mary; and/or numerous "saints"; and/or the "Pope"; and/or the communion bread – amongst other things. By definition, this is idolatrous. Since Holy Scripture commands us to "flee from idolatry," no Christian can afford to cooperate in a religious way with Catholics.[46]

As illustrated in the chart, the Roman Catholics affected the mainstream philosophy, religious cults, secret societies, psychology/psychiatry, fortune-telling, necromancy, Pentecostal frenzies, miracles and prosperity gospel, seminary institutions, theological teachings, and even praise song lyrics to infiltrate deeply into the church practices with secular culture and demonic doctrines.

The Dragnet Behind Alpha, Vineyard, 'Purpose-Driven', 'Toronto' etc

•The key network underlying the Alpha Course before release in '92•

Each link represents admitted influence or open co-operation. As a minimum, believers really need to know about the names on the outer perimeter of this chart. See notes below for more.

Alpha Alpha Alpha

John Wimber
(/Vineyard)

C.Peter Wagner
David Pytches
Morton Kelsey
Richard Foster /Renovaré
John Bertolucci
John/Paula Sandford
Agnes Sanford
Charles Kraft
George Fox /Quakers
Ruth Carter-Stapleton
Francis MacNutt
Michael Scanlan

Fuller Seminary
Paul Cain/ 'KCProphets'
Ken Copeland /Ken Hagin Snr
Victor Paul Wierwille
William Branham /Latter Rainers
Lonnie Frisbee
Fort Lauderdale Five
Léon Joseph Suenens
Kathryn Kuhlman
Robert Schuller

Roberto Assag-ioli
Carl Jung
Jakob Boehm-e/Jane Leade
P.Teil-hard deChar-din

E.W. Ken-yon
Aimee Semple McPhe-rson
Frank-lin Hall
Free-mas-ons

Jesuits and other Roman Catholics

NOTES: (1) Catholicism is idolatrous. We must oppose, not legitimize, idolaters: 1 Cor. 5:11; 1 Tim. 6:3,5; 2 John 1:9-11; Eph. 5:11 etc. (2) The dark perimeter holds the most blatantly idolatrous entries (all can be traced to Rome too). Wimber was invariably just one step away, with two walls of names acting as a 'front' for the side entries. (3) Pre-1993 Vineyard links to HTB were legion! (4) For readability, some links coalesce into a single, thicker line. (5) The five italicized entries above also led directly to the 'anointing' of Hinn & RHB – the very men who then produced 'Toronto'. (6) Many, if not most, of these 166 links follow chronologically (and many are 2-way). (7) The seven underlined entries above also led directly to Rick Warren's ministry. (8) Given more space or time, one could add even more links, especially from Freemasons, and add other highly-interlinked names (plus many indirect/post-'92 links). (9) HTB now works directly with almost every extant name. (10) This degree of interconnection can be no coincidence. This is guilt by co-operation, not just by association. Indeed, beware this undeniable and ungodly alliance - and anyone else unrepentantly connected to this web. Visit the 'Rubies' part of bayith.org for colour copies of this chart plus details of all links and names. Bayith Ministries

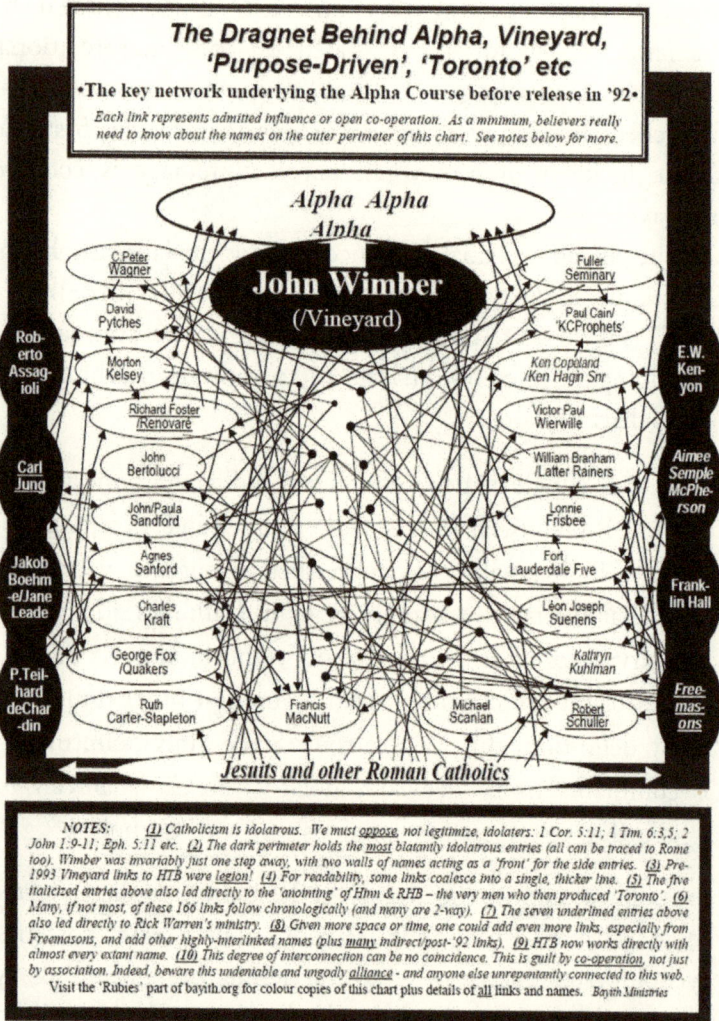

Fig. 5-1. Bayith Ministry Chart. [47]

At present, the rider of the white horse—the Catholic papacy—has already gone through the "conquering and to conquer" process and established itself as the powerhouse of seducing multitude of souls.

CHAPTER 6

THE THIRD SEAL: A YOKE

IS THE THIRD SEAL FAMINE?

The interpretation has revealed that the first seal occurred in 534 and the fourth seal started circa 1206–1227 as Genghis Khan built his empire during that period. Taking the interpretational principles into an account that the seals of Revelation are written sequentially and the historical incidents can, in fact, be interpreted in respective chronological order, the natural conclusion for the second and third seals is that they occurred sometime after 534 and before 1206.

Therefore, the two seals—the second and the third—would have opened in such way that the second would have occurred closer to the year of 534 and the third nearer to 1206. Then, what may be the third seal? The Scripture describes it as follows:

[Rev 6:5] And when he had opened the third seal, I heard the third beast say, Come and see. And I beheld, and lo a black horse; and he that sat on him had a pair of balances in his hand.

[Rev 6:6] And I heard a voice in the midst of the four beasts say, A measure of wheat for a penny, and three measures of barley for a penny; and see thou hurt not the oil and the wine.

This passage has been interpreted by a majority of scholars to be *famine* for the following reasons: 1) the presence of a rider of the horse with "a pair of balances in his hand" and 2) the reference to the price of "a measure of wheat for a penny," which scholars thought to be caused by the rising crop price during famine that made the lives of ordinary people difficult.

Furthermore, the scholars have linked this passage to the events Jesus had spoken about that would unfold in the last days, and many interpreted this passage of the third seal to correspond to the famine in the following Scriptures:

[Mt 24:5] For many shall come in my name, saying, I am Christ; and shall deceive many.

[Mt 24:6] And ye shall hear of wars and rumours of wars: see that ye be not troubled: for all these things must come to pass, but the end is not yet.

[Mt 24:7] For nation shall rise against nation, and kingdom against kingdom: and there shall be *famines*, and pestilences, and earthquakes, in divers places.

[Mt 24:8] All these are the beginning of sorrows.

From the passage above, many matched the "deception" with the first seal, the "wars and rumors of wars" to be the second seal, the "famines" as the third seal, and the "pestilences" the fourth. Jesus had warned believers that these events will occur in the last days, as written in Matthew 24. Jesus' warnings in

Matthew 24 are given significant attention by many believers, and many are convinced that He is speaking of Daniel's final seventieth week, the last seven years of mankind, in this passage. Consequently, most believers conclude that all of the first to fourth seals will occur during the last seven years of mankind. (Details on Daniel's seventieth week will be discussed in later volumes.)

Based on the interpretations so far in the previous chapters, however, the third seal would not occur during the last seven years, but sometime after 534 and before 1206. Yet, matching the events in Matthew 24 sequentially with the seals in Revelation in respective order seemed fairly reasonable. Therefore, search was carried out on the famines between the sixth and twelfth centuries.

Initial research began on the web, searching for any reference to famines during the relevant period. The result revealed that famines were relatively prevalent during the eleventh century compared to other era in history.

YEAR	LOCATION	EFFECT
1016	Europe	
1051	Mexico (present day)	Migration of the Toltecs
1064–1072	Egypt	
1097	France	Plague

Table 6-1. Famines in the 11th century.[1]

The initial findings shown in the table seemed very satisfactory, as they seemed to agree with the sequential and chronological interpretational principles of Revelation.

However, suspicions arose before long. This interpretation—
the third seal represents famines—has been standing for a
long time, but it was probably incorrect. The reasoning was as
follows:

Famines were frequent, but severity was a different matter.
Even if it seemed famines occurred frequently in the eleventh
century, much of the information on famines prior to the
eleventh century may have been unavailable because the older
incidents dating in the first millennium were less preserved on
record. Furthermore, major famines existed before the eleventh
century also, but the accounts at that time rarely reported how
many had died from the famines.

But what was more peculiar is the fact that John readily
used the word "famine" in the fourth seal.

[Rev 6:8] And I looked, and behold a pale horse: and
his name that sat on him was Death, and Hell followed
with him. And power was given unto them over the
fourth part of the earth, to kill with sword, and with
hunger, and with death, and with the beasts of the earth.

The word "hunger" in the above passage on the fourth seal
is λιμός (*limos*) in the original text which is the identical word
Jesus spoke of in Matthew 24:7 referring to famines. Hence,
should the third seal truly be referring to famines, John should
have used the word λιμός (*limos*) to specifically refer to famines.
This begs for an answer: why wouldn't John use the word
"famine" to describe famine in the third seal? Although the
fourth seal contains several means of mass destruction—sword,
hunger, death, and beast—it still plainly lists famine (hunger)
as famine. Then, why can't "famine" be used to describe the
third seal if it actually refers to famine?

[Rev 6:5b] And I beheld, and lo a black horse; and he that sat on him had a pair of balances in his hand.

[Rev 6:6b] A measure of wheat for a penny, and three measures of barley for a penny; and see thou hurt not the oil and the wine.

Next, if this was really a famine, and if oil and wine were not to be "hurt," or affected by the famine, would wheat and barley be scarcely produced or consumed in a region while oil and wine are produced or consumed abundantly in the same region? Was this even reasonable, let alone its possibility?

With common sense, this question didn't seem to make sense, because famines would commonly affect all four crops. Instinct dictated that if wheat and barley were to be produced in a region, oil and wine probably could be produced as well. And if oil and wine were consumed plentifully, wheat and barley would have been readily available as well.

Furthermore, a country or nation wouldn't have chosen to cultivate only grains over vineyards or vice versa, especially during the old times where trading was not as efficient and effective as today. From this perspective, it became more plausible that the third seal may not be about famine.

With this conclusion established, the next search began with the areas that produce wheat and barley and to see if they are grown in the same region. The regions producing wheat and barley are similar.[2] Although the research was pertinent to the producing regions of modern days, considering how the crop yields is closely related to the climate and the soil, it was speculated that the overlap of regions producing these two crops may not differ drastically even in different epochs. If so, the regions would have looked somewhat comparable even in tenth to twelfth centuries.

The regions that produce both wheat and barley as major crops are Canada and Alaska, Northern Europe, Western Europe, Southern Europe, Eastern Europe, European Russia, Asiatic Russia, Northern Africa, the Middle East, Central Asia, and Australia/New Zealand.[3]

Among these regions, the tenth-century Canada and Alaska, Asiatic Russia, Central Asia, and Australia/New Zealand regions may be ruled out for consideration since they lack recorded Bible-significant customs and incidents. However, readers will discover how other regions, including America, eventually appear in the unfolding of historical incidents in the seals and trumpets of Revelation. Henceforth, the regions that require scrutiny are limited to Northern Europe, Western Europe, Southern Europe, Eastern Europe, European Russia, Northern Africa, and the Middle East.

The next question was whether the oil and wine producing regions overlap with the wheat and barley producing regions. If the oil and wine producing regions do not produce much wheat and barley, then it would add to the perplexity of interpreting the third seal. Consequently, the search was done to look for oil and wine producing regions.

According to *Thayer's Greek-English Lexicon*, the "oil" in the passage is ἔλαιον (*elaion*), which, at the time it was written in the Bible, was used for feeding lamps, namely *olive oil*.[4] Duly, the regions producing the olives needed to be examined. Furthermore, the "wine" comes from *grapes*, and correspondingly, regions growing grapes were surveyed.

Research showed that the regions that produce both olives and grapes are Southern Europe and the Middle East.[5] But to one's surprise, wheat and barley were also the major crops of these two regions. The Bible seemed to indicate for the third seal that the price of wheat and barley were heavily affected while oil and wine remained intact, which connoted the likelihood of the region(s) producing all four kinds—not only wheat and barley but also oil and wine.

Even though the expression "hurt not the oil and the wine" was not understood at this point, it seemed certain that the affected regions of the third seal produced oil and wine as well as wheat and barley. Decisively, in the third seal, the Bible was clearly speaking of an event that happened in a region that was related to wheat, barley, oil, and wine. Therefore, further investigation concentrated on the Southern Europe and the Middle East regions.

In order to understand the third seal event, it was inevitable to ponder over the question: what does it mean by "not to hurt the oil and the wine"? If olive and grapes were produced, why were they not "hurt"? What does it mean by "hurt"?

[Rev 6:6b] and see thou *hurt* not the oil and the wine.

The word "hurt" in the verse is ἀδικέω (*adikeō*) in Greek which is defined as follows:[6]

Meaning:

1) absolutely

    a   to act unjustly or wickedly, to sin

    b   to be a criminal, to have violated the laws in some way

    c   to do wrong

    d   to do hurt

2) transitively

    a   to do some wrong or sin in some respect

b   to wrong someone, act wickedly towards him

c   to hurt, damage, harm

The word ἀδικέω (*adikeō*) comes from the root word ἄδικος (*adikos*), meaning "unjust, unrighteous, or sinful."[7] This probably means that some people were not allowed access to oil and wine, and if they attempted to possess or consume oil or wine, then such act must have been deemed "sinful, unrighteous, and violating" the prohibitive regulation.

Understanding this aspect of the definition of "hurt" prompted an inquiry on whether there was such a political or societal discrimination against a group of people before the thirteenth century.

The quest to resolve this inquiry was initiated by asking the question: Why "a pair of balances?" This "pair of balances" naturally makes one relate the third seal to rationing scarce food supplies. This description seemed to fit both situations: 1) a famine-induced rationing of food, which proved an incorrect and improbable interpretation, as the third seal is not about famine; and 2) since it was not allowed to violate the domain of the oil and the wine, the pair of balances was only employed to regulate the access to wheat and barley against a group of people.

However, these strings of words still rendered enigmatic even from its context. From what is known so far, there is presumably a region where wheat, barley, olives, and grapes are produced, and in that region, there must have been some kind of system regulating the price of the produced wheat and barley so that they were offered at a high price to the laborers of that region, while olives and grapes were systematically made inaccessible to the producing laborers.

What is more, wheat and barley were measured on a pair of balances, meaning they were to be distributed only in allotted amounts in Revelation 6:6. If this were the case of famine, then the olives and the grapes could not be in profusion, and their prices would have skyrocketed. However, the Scripture does not include the price of olives and grapes. Regardless of the abundance, something forbids the access to oil and wine to certain people. Such interpretation reaffirms that the passage is not speaking of famine.

In order to fully make sense of the event described in the third seal, the verses were scrutinized word by word in the original Greek text. And this led to an interesting discovery regarding the phrase "a pair of balances."

[Rev 6:5b] And I beheld, and lo a black horse; and he that sat on him had *a pair of balances* in his hand.

The word translated as "a pair of balances" in original Greek is ζυγός (*zygos*), which appears 6 times in the Scriptures. Its definition is as follows:[8]

Meaning:

1) a yoke

   a   a *yoke* that is put on draught cattle

   b   metaph., used of any burden or *bondage*

- as that of slavery

- of troublesome laws imposed on one, esp. of the Mosaic law, hence the name is so transferred to the commands of Christ as to contrast them with the commands of the Pharisees which were a veritable 'yoke'; yet even Christ's

commands must be submitted to, though
easier to be kept
2) a *balance*, pair of scales

Note that this word ζυγός (*zygos*) metaphorically denotes *bondage* as that of slavery. It is translated as "*yoke*" in five places in the Bible, and only once in this Revelation passage as "a pair of balances." The five verses where "yoke" is used for translation are as follows:

[Mt 11:29] Take my *yoke* upon you, and learn of me; for I am meek and lowly in heart: and ye shall find rest unto your souls.

[Mt 11:30] For my *yoke* is easy, and my burden is light.

[Ac 15:10] Now therefore why tempt ye God, to put a *yoke* upon the neck of the disciples, which neither our fathers nor we were able to bear?

[Gal 5:1] Stand fast therefore in the liberty wherewith Christ hath made us free, and be not entangled again with the *yoke* of bondage.

[1 Ti 6:1] Let as many servants as are under the *yoke* count their own masters worthy of all honour, that the name of God and his doctrine be not blasphemed.

Among all usages in the Bible, ζυγός (*zygos*) was used as "a pair of balances" only once, in Revelation! In retrospect, ζυγός (*zygos*) was probably translated into "a pair of balances" in Revelation because the translators interpreted the passage to be a famine with the prices of grains in context in mind.

IS THE THIRD SEAL SLAVERY?

The fact that this "pair of balances" is actually used as a "yoke" throughout the Scriptures serves as a basis for translating the expression in Revelation 6:5 as "yoke," possibly to refer to a slavery or bondage system. Verse 5 would actually read, "And I beheld, and lo a black horse; and he that sat on him had a *yoke* in his hand."

It should be reinforced at this point that the seals occur in centurial intervals. Another important characteristic of seals is that they have lasting effects throughout history. Once a seal is opened, its artifacts and cultural remains tend to continue for a long time, often to this date. This effect was noticeable as interpretation of each seal was being completed one by one, as the historical incidents corresponding to the seals were significant milestones in history. Certainly, most of them had been discussed in history classes, such that any non-historians would easily recognize them.

This lasting effect is similar to that of slavery which has been a prevalent component of human history. Ever since the first form of slavery existed, all kinds of slavery have existed to this date—sex trafficking, plantation slavery, child labor, miners, and so on. In interpreting of the third seal, the possibility of the "yoke" being *slavery* was weighed, knowing the gravity of tragic trails that slavery had left in human history.

But was this interpretation correct? Probably not, for reasons discussed next. Examining the history of slavery confirmed that the third seal was not slavery.

Living in the information age has an immense advantage in being able to look up pretty much any information needed and confirm it. For instance, a table of death toll such as *Possibly the 20 Worst Things People Have Done to Each Other* shows how much of an impact slavery had in world history. From the top

20 list, the eighth, *the Mideast Slave Trade*, caused 18.5 million deaths.[9]

The Middle East slave trade, or the slavery in the Islamic world, dates from the seventh century, as early as the year 650. The number of African slaves through trans-Saharan slave trade from 650–1600 is estimated as 4,820,000, and through the Red Sea and East African slave trade from 800–1600 as 2,400,000.[10] Other estimates of Islam's African slaves range from 11.5 million to 14 million.[11]

The truth is, none can ascertain how many African slaves were sold since the seventh-century slavery trade. But needless to say, certainly a prodigious number of slaves were traded. Then, could the third seal be referring to the rampant trading of these slaves?

[Rev 6:6b] *A measure of wheat for a penny, and three measures of barley for a penny*; and see thou hurt not the oil and the wine.

Contemplating the Scripture again, approaching the third seal as slavery lead to a bigger conundrum. If the third seal in fact referred to slavery and the verse states "a measure of wheat for a penny," could slaves be paying money for their food? Intuition bid they wouldn't be. One wouldn't expect slaves to store cash for themselves. It seemed counterintuitive for anyone who can pay for food to be a slave. So the third seal may not have been about slavery after all.

If it was not about slavery, then Northern Africa should be definitely excluded from consideration for the third seal. To move forward, Southern Europe and the Middle East were compared to see which of these two regions grew and distributed the four crops.

In Southern Europe, wheat takes up 21.0 percent of all crop distributed, barley 16.1 percent, olives 15.1 percent, and grapes 9.4 percent, while in the Middle East, wheat constitutes 43.4 percent, barley 21.0 percent, grapes 2.6 percent, and olives 2.2 percent.[12] Indisputably, the analysis reveals that relatively fewer olives and grapes are produced from the Middle East. Thus, it is more than safe to conclude that the major yield of these four crops comes from Southern Europe. Not only that, these four crops are considered Mediterranean region's basic crops.[13]

For example, in ancient Greece, "the main crops were barley, grapes, and olives. Grain crops, such as barley and wheat, were planted in October and harvested in April or May. Olives were harvested November through February. Grapes were normally picked in September. Barley was the main cereal crop for the ancient Greek farmers . . . Olive oil was used for cooking oil or in oil lamps. Grapes were primarily used for wine production, although they could be eaten or dried into raisins."[14] On the grounds of the abovementioned, Southern Europe was most likely the region related to the third seal.

Another fact to bear in mind was that olive oil and wine are secondary products of olives and grapes. Did not God write "wheat and barley" instead of the "bread made from wheat and barley?" But for olive oil, God did not write "olive trees"; and for wine, He did not write "grape trees."

Why so? This is clearly referring to the olive oil and the wine that first come from olive trees and grape trees, respectively, then through certain manufacturing process are produced and transported for consumption in other wider regions. This suggests the possibility that the regions concerned in the third seal not only produce wheat and barley but also consume olive oil and wine on a regular basis, possibly imported.

Although the region producing wheat, barley, olives, and grapes has already been examined and specified, that region was merely a portion referred to in the third seal. The third seal, as have been addressed previously, probably not only concerned Southern Europe but also other regions that consume imported olive oils and wine.

However, the restriction that such region must produce wheat and barley still remains effective. In addition, the regions that not only grew wheat and barley but also imported olive oil and wine that were produced from Southern Europe in the tenth to twelfth centuries must have been primarily within Europe.

As will be further expanded upon later, one of the factors that restricted the trading of olive oil and wine to the intra-Europe region was the Arab conquests in the Mediterranean by the Middle Eastern Muslim forces during the seventh century. All things considered, the third seal was speculated to have been centered in Europe.

To understand the Scriptures in depth, the next thing to delve into was, "how much are 'a measure of wheat for a penny' and 'three measures of barley for a penny'?"

[Mt 20:2] And when he had agreed with the labourers for *a penny* a day, he sent them into his vineyard.

The word "*penny*" here is originally δηνάριον (*dēnarion*), and it is interpreted as the ordinary pay for a day's wages for a laborer.[15] Therefore, the passage in Revelation 6:6 has something to do with the laborers and their wages, and it possibly implies that laborers were working very hard all day long, yet only to receive a measure of wheat or three measures of barley for a day's work.

[Rev 6:6b] *A measure of wheat* for a penny, and *three measures of barley* for a penny; and see thou hurt not the oil and the wine.

The word "measure" here is originally χοῖνιξ (*choinix*), which means: "a dry measure, containing four cotylae or two setarii (less than our quart, one litre) (or as much as would support a man of moderate appetite for a day)."[16]

According to the *Commentary on the Old and New Testaments* by Robert Jamieson, A. R. Fausset, and David Brown, "a measure" is "about a day's provision of wheat, variously estimated at two or three pints," and "for a penny or denarius," which is about "eight and a half pence of our money," signifies probably the day's wages of a laborer.[17]

Another commentary on the terms "measure" and "penny" writes:

A measure of wheat for a penny - The word rendered "measure" - χοῖνιξ (*choinix*) - denotes an Attic measure for grain and things dry, equal to the 48th part of the Attic medimnus, or the 8th part of the Roman modius, and consequently was nearly equivalent to one quart English. The word rendered "penny", δηναρίον (*dēnarion*) - Latin, denarius - was of the same value as the Greek δραχμή (*drachmē*), and was equivalent to about fourteen cents or seven-pence (circa mid-19th century). This was the usual price of a day's labor, Mt 20:2, Mt 20:9. The choenix, or measure of grain here referred to, was the ordinary daily allowance for one man. The common price of the Attic medimnus of wheat was five or six denarii; but here, as that contained

48 choenixes or quarts, the price would be augmented to 48 denarii - or *it would be about eight times as dear as ordinary.*[18]

And another commentary testifies that the wheat price had inflated eight times the ordinary price.[19]

To reiterate, the laborers deserved to get paid eight times more of wheat as daily wage compared to what is stated in Rev 6:6. In the situation of the third seal, the laborer's earning was only limited to one measure of wheat for his day's labor.

In 1315, when the Great Famine put Europe into turmoil, records indicate that wheat price sored up to 400 percent.[20] It is probable that in times of severe famine the price could have soared even higher. In general, during times of famine, the price of wheat and barley would skyrocket as the famine is prolonged further.

In the third seal, however, the circumstance is different. The prices of wheat and barley are fixed according to the Scripture, which indicates that these prices are not altered for a long time. Thus, this unequivocal piece of information definitively affirms the third seal is not about famine. The inflated price in the third seal is fixed for a long term and probably arises from a social structure. Such price inflation may even yield tougher livelihood than in times of famine.

Nevertheless, the majority of commentaries go along with the interpretation of the third seal being a famine. But for all the abovementioned reasons, the third seal is not and cannot be famine. So, if it is not famine, and it is not slavery, then what is it?

THE FEUDAL SYSTEM

Suppose there is a laborer who gets paid per day, yet his wage can only purchase the basic crop at a price eight times higher than the normal price, and he is restricted from the privilege to access luxurious items such as oil and wine.

In the third seal, the Bible is portraying such a poverty-stricken form of slavery languishing under such gruesome rights-deprived condition. Such circumstance describes a form of labor abuse but is somewhat different from a pure form of slavery. Slaves are the properties of the owner and do not get paid per day.

Hence, the rights-deprived laborers of the third seal are not slaves but a socioeconomic group that are sweated and exploited systematically like slaves. A thorough examination of medieval European history identified such exploitation system to be the "serfdom" under "feudalism."

The practice of feudalism was first seen in France and Germany in the ninth and tenth centuries. The system reproduced that of the fallen Roman Empire in the fifth century, in which Romans used to affiliate themselves with loyal soldiers and fighting force for protection. Coupled with these remnants of Roman elements, European nobles augmented their power further through endowments of lands from the King in exchange for military service. In this fashion, feudalism was impregnated and spread throughout Europe.[21]

Meanwhile in the seventh century in the Middle East, the Islamic prophet Muhammad had risen to conquer beyond the Arabian Peninsula as far as the borders of China and India to the east and as far as Northern Africa to the west, and even the Iberian Peninsula during the eighth century. This Islamic expansion is called the "Islamic conquests" or "Arab conquests."[22]

This spread of Muslim power dismantled the trade across the Mediterranean and eventually eradicated all long-distance trade, leaving the Western Europe to regress to an isolated, stagnant, and subsistent agrarian economy (refer to Fig. 6-1). Ergo, some argue that feudalism was widely spread in Europe circa tenth century.[23]

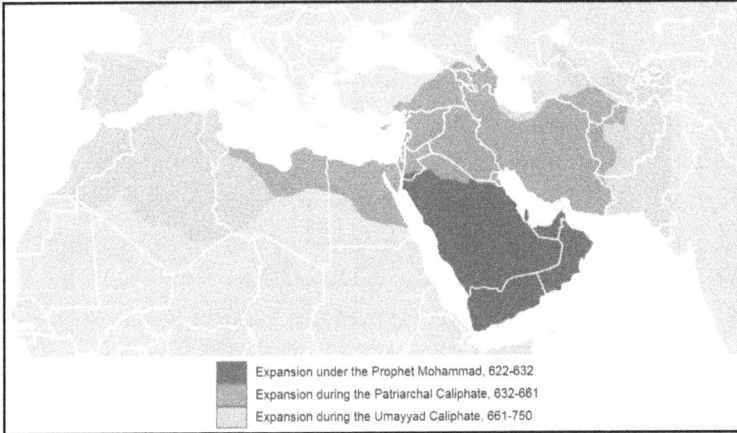

Expansion under the Prophet Mohammad, 622-632
Expansion during the Patriarchal Caliphate, 632-661
Expansion during the Umayyad Caliphate, 661-750

Fig. 6-1. Expansion of the Caliphates.[24]

Labor exploitation prevailed in the European feudal society in the name of serfdom, which refers to the "condition in medieval Europe in which a tenant farmer was bound to hereditary plot of land and to the will of his landlord."[25] Serfs maintained their subsistence by cultivating a field of land owned by lords and paying their dues to their landlords. The difference between serfs and slaves were that slaves were not tied to the land and could be sold and bought in a trade.[26] This system was employed even to the extent that the aristocrats, as well as monasteries, through their legal power over them, demanded serfs' labor on their land without pay. This is defined in the history as "manorialism."[27]

As the lowest group of the feudal social hierarchy, serfs were legally, economically, and socially bound to their lords. While serfs labored on the manors they were bound to, they did not possess any rights to the property or the produce they harvested. Such status of bondage could be interpreted as a modified slavery, which took its prime during High Middle Ages, and in certain parts of the world lasted until the mid-nineteenth century.

Serfs bound to a land served their landowners, and in return, received protection from the owners. The relationship between a serf and his landowner was initiated and solidified through two ceremonies. The first one was called "homage," in which gestures and declarations were made to present the establishment of the serf's submissive role to his lord. In the second one, which was an "oath of fealty" that included a religious component, the serf swore his faithful service to his lord.[28] Their "oath of fealty" read:

> By the Lord before whom this sanctuary is holy, I will to N. be true and faithful, and love all which he loves and shun all which he shuns, according to the laws of God and the order of the world. Nor will I ever with will or action, through word or deed, do anything which is unpleasing to him, on condition that he will hold to me as I shall deserve it, and that he will perform everything as it was in our agreement when I submitted myself to him and chose his will.[29]

The homage ceremony was always accompanied by an oath of fealty, both of which rendered the "personal bondage (*homage de corps*)" of the serf to his landowner official in feudal contract until death of either party.[30]

Once bound to their landowners, serfs had to pay service or dues to their lords in cash, produce, labor, or any combination of them. In addition, serfs were not allowed to move permanently or marry without their lord's approval. Virtually all aspects of a serf's life were committed in service to his lord. This "bondage" of serfdom was even inherited to the serf's descendants.[31]

Despite the restricted freedom that encompassed the lifestyle of a serf bound to a land and its owner, serfs differed from slaves in that serfs were able to have money. With their money, serfs paid rent or taxes to their lords, and even bought their freedom with an amount large enough to purchase a plot of land. They worked for their lords Mondays through Saturdays, and also worked on the pieces of land provided by their lords to feed their family, living a life of travail.[32]

A serf, with most of his freedom surrendered to his lord, was bound to the land he lived in for life. This "bondage" that prevailed throughout feudal Europe was the very thing that Bible mentions with the word "ζυγός (zygos)," meaning "yoke or bondage," not "a pair of balances." This "bondage" made serfs commit most of their working hours to serving their lords and work additional hours for their own subsistence, thus paying a significant amount of labor for their basic needs.

Serfdom came to an end with the Renaissance in Western Europe and other circumstances such as the Black Death that reached Europe in 1347. With the significant reduction in population due to the bubonic plague, various kinds of labor were in much higher demand. People started to pay laborers higher prices for their services, nullifying the submissive positions of serfs and placing their values much higher.[33]

FEUDALISM IN ENGLAND

Investigating the feudal system in England allows deeper understanding of the economic situation in the Middle Ages. King William I (the Conqueror) ordered documentation of all properties of landowners, including those of inhabitants of all manors, throughout the nation around 1086. Detailed survey of all lands were recorded and published in the *Domesday Book*, which provides substantial insight into the English economics of that time.[34] The record, therefore, details virtually all aspects of England's feudalism at the time.

During the Middle Ages harvest of crops was difficult. For the amount of seeds used to sow, at most only a quadruple of the amount were reaped. Compared to modern-day agriculture, three times more land was needed back then for the same amount of harvest. While two acres of wheat planted fed one person per year on average, peasant households were provided on average twelve to fifteen acres in the fourteenth century. Peasants with lower socioeconomic status most often had maximum five acres of land from which to feed themselves, and they had to labor in order to earn sufficient wage for survival.[35] As they usually had ten members in each family, their economic situation was arduous year-round.[36]

In order to appreciate economic system in feudal societies, understanding the social hierarchy in England is important. The king and the nobles were at the top of the hierarchy, and the nobles included senior churchmen and barons. Those at the top hierarchical category were the ruling elite of England, who owned approximately three quarters of all land in England. The next in hierarchy were knights, who earned their status through service or through wealth. In addition to the two hundred nobles that formed the ruling elite, there were one thousand knights by the fourteenth century. Next in hierarchy were *sokemen* freemen, who formed one sixth of England's population and owned roughly one fifth of the land. They inherited their land, for which they paid fixed rent with income earned through light labor or service.[37]

The rest of the population constituted of serfs who were at the bottom of the hierarchy. Serfs were also divided into levels of socioeconomic status, with the highest and largest class being villeins, the middle being bordars and cottars, and the lowest being slaves. Villeins formed a little less than half of England's population, and the area of farmland they worked on was almost half of all lands in the nation. The villeins were allowed to work on their lords' lands by providing them with labor. Bordars and cottars formed as much as a third of England's population but worked on only five percent of all land in the nation and had to pay rent or labor for use.[38]

A little less than ten percent of the population was slaves, who had no land to work on. However, serfs' socioeconomic statuses could change between different levels. Those who saved up wealth purchased lands while free men could become villeins, and slaves received holdings that allowed them to become bordars.[39]

Over time, the population grew and more peasants became free. As a result, not enough crops were harvested to feed the rising population, and peasants ended up holding less land and their wage was reduced. Serfs who were usually paid per day had to offer their services for payment per task. By the year 1300, this competition among serfs for rendering low-wage labor eventually removed slavery from the social hierarchy, and serfs were evenly distributed among villeins, bordars and cottars.[40]

It is noteworthy to point out that serfs were paid per day for most of feudal era. At the end of a day's work, they were paid a wage for the day, rather than for the task. This fact corresponds to the word δηναρίον (*dēnarion;* penny or denarius) God specifically uses to describe the third seal with, as it categorically signifies a laborer's day's wage.

LIFE OF THE SERFS

Under the feudal system, serfs had much of their personal freedom taken away, including the selection of their spouse. Any disagreement with the owner would incur fines on the serfs.[41]

In any work including harvesting, priority was given to the lord's over serf's. Serfs also had to dig ditches, gather firewood, build and fix fences, and repair roads and bridges, which were the services that were mostly rendered for their lord. In addition, serfs had to pay taxes to their lords for their own existence, property, inheritance, and use of their lord's property for labor rendered to their lords.[42]

In medieval England, peasants paid ten percent of all their farm produce as tax to the church. While the church increased its collection of produce in huge barns, this ten percent in taxation was enough to cause financial crisis in many peasants' households and serious shortage of seeds for next sowing season as well as feeding themselves.[43]

> [Rev 6:6] . . . A measure of wheat for a penny, and three measures of barley for a penny; . . .

"A measure of wheat for a penny" denotes that a penny (δηναρίον, *dēnarion*) was a serf's pay for the day and that a serf was only paid a measure of wheat per day. This wage for serfs was a severely discounted rate compared to the wage paid to other classes of freemen. In other words, serfs were exploited of their labor in return for protection, justice, and rights to toil in the manor's fields but only allowed to survive at a subsistence level.

FOOD FOR THE SERFS

As the Scripture for the third seal mentions wheat, barley, oil, and wine, food culture during the Middle Ages was explored. Since ancient times, the main staple food around the Mediterranean was cereal, especially a variety of cuisine made of wheat. During the Middle Ages, bread made with wheat, barley, and rye was the basic food. Flour was made from these grains at the landowner's mill. White flour was prepared for the nobles with fine grinding and brown flour was prepared for the peasants. The poor ate bread made of barley, rye, and oat flour. The nobles, on the contrary, enjoyed bread made of wheat.[44]

Throughout the medieval era, dependence on wheat was substantial and the reliance spread from Southern to Northern Europe. In colder climates, wheat was harder to obtain and therefore was only affordable by higher classes.[45] These records suggest that the price of wheat must have been higher than that of barley during the Middle Ages, which is what the Scripture writes.

[Rev 6:6] . . . A measure of wheat for a penny, and three measures of barley for a penny; . . .

Meat was also prestigious food only available to the nobility or to poachers, because pork, chicken, and other domestic fowl required greater investment in land, thus making it more expensive.[46]

Foreign spices and exotic imported foods were also common only to the nobility, since the inefficient long-distance transportation and food preservation techniques inflated the cost. Therefore, the value of olive oil and wine was comparable and they were available to the privileged classes in regions that do not grow olives or grapes:[47]

In the British Isles, northern France, the Low Countries, the northern German-speaking areas, Scandinavia and the Baltic the climate was generally too harsh for the cultivation of grapes and olives. In the south, wine was the common drink for both rich and poor alike (though the commoner usually had to settle for cheap second pressing wine) while beer was the commoner's drink in the north and wine an expensive import… Olive oil was a ubiquitous ingredient around the Mediterranean, but remained an expensive import in the north where oil of poppy, walnut, hazel and filbert was the most affordable alternative.[48]

As the Scriptures write, the serfs provided labor at a very cheap price. The lower classes mainly consumed barley, and wheat remained as the preferred victuals for nobler classes. The phrase "see thou hurt not the oil and the wine" indicates the olive oil and the wine were only accessible to the high classes because they were expensive import goods outside the shores of the Mediterranean. Fitly, the Scriptures accurately depict the life of the unfree and the poor slaving under the medieval feudal system.

The olive oil and the wine are made from olive tree and vine, respectively. The Bible clearly writes "hurt not the oil and the wine" instead of "hurt not the olive trees and the grape vines." This specific description points out there are two discrete classes of rich ruling nobles and servile serfs.

DECLINE OF FEUDALISM

Intriguingly, the feudalistic socioeconomic structure of the Middle Ages was brought to an end by none other than divine intervention. As the rise of the dichotomy between the nobility and the serfs was prophesied in Revelation's third seal, the fall of the feudalism was also initiated by the fourth seal, as seen in the following excerpt:

> The Crisis of the Late Middle Ages marked by economic crisis and series of famines and plagues in first place by the Great Famine of 1315–17 and the Black Death in the 1340s, greatly affected all classes of feudal society, including the peasants. Reduced rural population, increased need for wage workers, and a series of peasants' revolts eventually led to weakening of serfdom, which virtually disappeared in Western Europe by the end of the Late Middle Ages.[49]

CAPITALISM AND LABOR EXPLOITATION

According to Karl Marx, feudalism served as the basis for eventual birth of capitalism:

> The economic structure of capitalistic society has grown out of the economic structure of feudal society. The dissolution of the latter set free the elements of the former . . . The starting-point of the development that gave rise

to the wage-labourer as well as to the capitalist, was the servitude of the labourer. The advance consisted in a change of form of this servitude, in the transformation of feudal exploitation into capitalist exploitation.[50]

In other words, the third seal does not stop simply with the end of the feudalism, but its ramification continues on to the creation of modern capitalism. Every opening of a seal has its critical lasting aftereffects in history. For example, the first seal that legally established the rights of papacy has continual effect as the pope in modern days assumes a momentous role with supreme, global presence. In the case of the fourth seal also, the western expansion of Genghis Khan had an eventual ripple effect in bridging the Oriental with the West culturally and commercially.

Taken together, the third seal spells out the feudalism and the serfdom that commenced in the tenth century. The feudalism eventually gave rise to the modern style of capitalistic labor exploitation, and continuation of such exploitive system initiated from feudalism has far-reaching impact in today's socioeconomic structure.

CHAPTER 7

THE SECOND SEAL:
PEACE TAKEN FROM THE EARTH

IS THE SECOND SEAL A WAR?

The first seal was an event that gave the pope official authority to become "head of all the Holy churches" in the year 534. The third seal was feudalism that affected Europe during the tenth century. Now let us look into the second seal.

The second seal must have occurred between the first and third seals. Therefore, it must have occurred after 534 and before the start of tenth century.

> [Rev 6:3] And when he had opened the second seal, I heard the second beast say, Come and see.

> [Rev 6:4] And there went out another horse that was red: and power was given to him that sat thereon to take peace from the earth, and that they should kill one another: and there was given unto him a great sword.

Many interpret that Rev 6:3–4 describes a war in the second seal. If this is true, then it would be natural to look into wars that occurred between seventh and ninth centuries. To do so, atrocious wars in history that incurred the highest death tolls were investigated.

Research revealed a large war that occurred between the seventh and ninth centuries, the An Shi Rebellion in China during the eighth century. Its death toll is estimated to be 36 million.[1] Yet, whether this incident actually was such an atrocious incident is unknown, as the estimated death toll may not be reliable.[2]

Would the second seal be a war? It could be so. However, interpretations have shown that seals bear lasting effects throughout history. These effects are possible as the seals actually are the primary or prototypical events that occur for the first time or in an unprecedentedly large scale. The seals in Revelation not only bear historical or phenomenal significance, but also give birth to ideas, philosophies, or systems that affect humanity even until today. Therefore, An Shi Rebellion, although a significant war of the eighth century, is merely one of many wars in history and may not be a historically symbolic incident from the apocalyptic perspective.

Some may also argue that the fact that Christianity had been introduced to China in the seventh century may be noteworthy. However, it is questionable as to whether China would have become such a significant place to be the stage for an event in the Bible at that time.

To see why China is unlikely the location of the second seal, let us discuss the seals interpreted so far. The significance of the first seal was in the emergence of false prophets. As Jesus has warned, false prophets will also be present in the last days. Note, however, that this seal was geographically centered around Europe, especially Rome.

The significance of the third seal was in feudalistic abuse of labor and high taxation under serfdom. This ideology has highly influenced the formation of capitalism. Most societies are immersed in this lifestyle even to this day. The geographical arena toward which the seal unrolled extends to the entire European continent.

In the fourth seal were war, famine, and pestilence. These phenomena continued to exist and affect humanity on a global level. Note how the seal expanded to even wider geographic locations as it included not only Europe but also the Asian continent.

The seals seem to record the phenomena, science, ideology, or -isms that occur as the first of its kind in history or on an unprecedentedly large scale with its features and artifacts recurring throughout history with varying intensity and forms until Jesus Christ returns. As each seal is opened, it gradually involved a wider geographic area in general. Considering this point, it seemed unlikely that China would suddenly become the stage where the second seal unraveled. Rather, the places adjacent to and in the vicinity of Rome, the stage of the first seal, seemed more plausible.

An exception to the expansion of involved geographic areas with the opening of seals was in the case of the fifth seal. The fifth seal, as will be discussed in the next chapter, has a special characteristic to the event that restricts it to a particular area of the world. As the fifth seal involves physical death of certain groups of people within a religio-political area, the geographic expansion of seal seems not to be applicable. In the remaining seals yet to be discussed in this book, however, geographic expansion was observed. The sixth seal showed that the regions in the prophecy finally included America. The effects of the seventh seal event reverberated around Earth two times in the form of seismic waves.

For these reasons, the An Shi Rebellion did not strike as the incident revealed in the second seal of Revelation. With the research results suggesting the possibility of the second seal not being a war and not being related to China, the Scripture needed to be better understood before further research could be attempted.

Reading the Scripture in its original Greek language revealed that the "sword" in Rev 6:4 was different from the "sword" used in the Mongol invasion of the fourth seal in Rev 6:8. The "sword" (ῥομφαία, *rhomphaia*) of the fourth seal was "a large sword"[3] used in wars and was used in other parts of Revelation only when describing Lord's "sharp sword with two edges" (Rev 2:12) and the sharp sword that came out of the Lord's mouth (Rev 1:16, 2:16, 19:15, 19:21). Genghis Khan used this sword (ῥομφαία, *rhomphaia*) in war to conquer the world.

In contrast, the "sword" in the second seal was μάχαιρα (*machaira*), which has two significant meanings. Its first meaning is "a large knife, used for killing animals and cutting up flesh" and second is "a small sword, as distinguished from a large sword."[4] To better understand the usage of this "sword," μάχαιρα (*machaira*), the Scriptures that use this particular word were reviewed. In the New Testament, this word was mostly used when someone had it to maintain public order or to harm another individual.

For example, the multitude that came to capture Jesus brought with them this "sword" (μάχαιρα, *machaira*) in Matthew 26:47. They came with this sword to capture the Lord as if they were after a thief (Mt 26:55). The sword Peter used to cut the right ear of the high priest's servant was this μάχαιρα (*machaira*) (Jn 18:10). When the keeper of prison in Philippi tried to kill himself thinking the prisoners had escaped, the sword he used was μάχαιρα (*machaira*) (Ac 16:27). In Romans 13, rulers of society bore the sword, μάχαιρα (*machaira*), in order to punish the evildoer (Ro 13:4). Also, the sword that slays the Antichrist before his wound is healed is μάχαιρα (*machaira*) (Rev 13:14). All of these were translated as "sword," but they can also be understood as a "large knife" or a "small sword." Overall, this sword is not used in wars, but in maintaining law and order or harming others on an individual level.

If the Scripture of the second seal was describing a war, the "sword" used should have been ῥομφαία (*rhomphaia*), which is used in wars. This is precisely why ῥομφαία (*rhomphaia*) was used in describing the fourth seal, the Mongol invasion. As the Scripture of the second seal uses μάχαιρα (*machaira*), not ῥομφαία (*rhomphaia*), the second seal does not describe a war.

In addition, in the second seal, there is only one event described, unlike the fourth seal, which involved war, famine, and pestilence. If the only event described in the second seal was a war, it is highly unlikely that μάχαιρα (*machaira*) would be used in Rev 6:4, as such sword is not used in war but in maintaining public law and order. Therefore, the second seal event does not describe a typical war.

Also, according to the Scripture, he that sat on the red horse received "a great sword" in the second seal. If the sword mentioned here is not the sword used in wars but the same kind as that Peter used to cut off the ear of high priest's servant (Jn 18:10), then no matter how "great" the sword is, it cannot be "greater" than the sword (ῥομφαία, *rhomphaia*) that Genghis Kahn used, assuming this greatness is measured in terms of size.

Why then does the Bible say that he was given "a great sword (μάχαιρα μεγάλη, *machaira megalē*)?" As the first meaning of the "sword" (*machaira*) is "a large knife," the expression "a great sword" may be literally referring to a large knife. If, however, a sword not used in war but merely used in maintaining public law or order was described as "great," is not the expression ironic? In other words, why was a relatively small sword described as "great?"

To answer this question, the word "great (μέγας, *megas*)" used in the Greek text was examined. This word does not only mean big in terms of shape and form, but also great in terms of intensity and degree. It is also used in describing "things esteemed highly for their importance."[5] Therefore, the Scripture may not necessarily signify that the sword is big in shape or form, but that the sword of the second seal has "great" impact.

Let us now look at the Scripture once again, now focusing on the word "kill."

[Rev 6:4] And there went out another horse that was red: and power was given to him that sat thereon to take *peace* from the earth, and that they should *kill* one another: and there was given unto him a great sword.

The Greek word "kill (σφάζω, *sphazō*)" means to slay, slaughter, or butcher, but it also means "to put to death by violence."[6] By inference, it is possible to argue that the meaning of this word includes the use of terror and violence as its means bringing death.

This word is used ten times in the New Testament. In all ten cases, this word is not used to mean "kill in war" but kill on an individual level. It was used when the Lord was killed (Rev 5:6, 9, 12, 13:8), when saints were killed (1Jn 3:12; Rev

6:9, 18:24), and when the Antichrist is wounded to death (Rev 13:3). It is apparent that this word is not used in war situations. Just as the sword (μάχαιρα, *machaira*) of the second seal is not used in wars, the word "kill" in this text also is used in homicidal situation, not in wars or massacres.

The word used to describe killing with the sword (ῥομφαία, *rhomphaia*) in the fourth seal was ἀποκτείνω (*apokteinō*), which is generally used to describe killing regardless of method.[7] This word was also used for killing in wars in the New Testament. For example, in the sixth trumpet in Revelation chapter 9, the third part of men is killed, and the word 'killed' is ἀποκτείνω (*apokteinō*) (Rev 9:15, 18, 20). It is also used in Revelation chapter 19 when people are "slain with the sword" in the last battle before the millennial kingdom (Rev 19:21).

Therefore, the words "sword" and "kill" in the second seal are not used in war situation. If the second seal is not referring to a war, then what is it referring to?

The next word to examine the definition and etymological origin was the word "peace," which is εἰρήνη (*eirēnē*) in Greek, in Revelation 6:4.

The first meaning of the word is "a state of national tranquility,"[8] an "exemption from rage and havoc of war."[9] What a concept! Is it not for this kind of national peace that Homeland Security, Department of Defense, Pentagon, and the United Nations exist? Is it not for this that a nation declares war on terror? Does not the TSA (Transportation Security Administration) raise control for body search in order to maintain this kind of state of peace?

The second definition of the word is "peace between individuals, as in harmony, concord," and the third meaning is "security, safety, prosperity, and felicity (as peace and harmony make and keep things safe and prosperous)."[10] The world might be crying out for security and prosperity on earth and for world peace, but there will be no true peace on earth until the King of Kings returns, if the second seal is about ridding the earth of peace and the effects continue to last afterwards.

When the second seal is opened, peace is taken away from the earth. 1 Thessalonians 5:3 states, "For when they shall say, Peace and Safety; then sudden destruction cometh upon them, as travail upon a woman with child; and they shall not escape." The "peace" used in this verse is also εἰρήνη (*eirēnē*). This verse implies that even toward the last days of mankind, nearing the return of Jesus Christ, "peace and safety" will still be an issue, whether on a regional, national, or global level. This is perhaps a lasting effect of the second seal, through which "peace" of certain level was taken away from the "earth."

Next, the meaning of the word "the earth" in this verse was reviewed. This word, "γῆ (*gē*; earth)" in Greek, usually refers to "arable land, ground, a standing place, main land as opposed to sea or water, or earth as a whole." Interestingly, it has another meaning, a "country, land enclosed within fixed boundaries, a tract of land, territory, region."[11]

So there it is! What if the word "earth (γῆ, *gē*)" was written to mean *land enclosed within fixed boundaries*? If "the earth" in the Scripture means *country* or nation, then when the prophecy is fulfilled, "peace" from the "earth," in terms of security—national security—will be taken away.

Of course, this would not be applied to nations only. As "the earth" refers to an area with fixed boundaries, if the area is local, then the peace would be taken away from the local area, and if the area is Europe, peace would be taken away from Europe.

Again, a seal refers to an event that continues to affect humanity until today since it had been opened. In the second seal, "the earth" refers to a region where the event occurred when a great sword was given unto him who sat on the red horse. If the opening of the second seal affects humanity until today, it is possible that the phenomenon of the second seal is seen today throughout a country, a local area, a continent, or the entire world. In short, the "great sword" given in the second seal clearly will manifest as an object of terror to nations as well as everyone living on Earth.

There is more evidence that shows that the second seal is not a war. The expression "one another" is ἀλλήλων (*allēlōn*) in Greek, which means "one another, reciprocally, and mutually."[12] This Greek word ἀλλήλων (*allēlōn*) was translated as "one another," "themselves," "yourselves," etc. in the King James Version Scriptures. In other words, this word was used when people affiliated with certain group or location shared a common activity or status. Being citizens of the same country falls into the category of being members of a group and sharing a common status. With the "earth" being a nation with fixed boundaries, the Scripture of the second seal may be suggesting fellow citizens of a country harming each other.

In a war, allied and enemy forces exist. Except in situations where allies and enemies are mixed together in a hand-to-hand combat, these two conflicting forces are usually clearly separated and distinct from each other in a war. The fact that ἀλλήλων (*allēlōn*) is used in the second seal shows that the event unfolded in the second seal is either a situation in which fellow citizens of the same country are harming each other or a situation in which allies and enemies are not distinguishable from each other.

What does it mean for people that are bonded together through citizenship or affiliation in a common group to harm each other with sword? What does it mean for people to harm each other with sword without conscious discrimination of whether their target is an ally or an enemy? What is clear is that the situation described in the second seal is not a war where ally and enemy forces are clearly distinguishable from each other.

RISE OF ISLAM

How might this peace be taken away from earth then? Revelation 6:3-4 seem to have something to do with "jihadism" in Islam as verse 4 particularly writes, "to take peace from the earth, and that they should kill one another." The reasoning for this conclusion is now explained.

With the definitions of the original Greek words in Revelation 6:4, the verse can be retranslated as: "And there went out another horse that was red: and power was given to him that sat thereon to take *security* from the *country* (*or some region, or the whole earth*), and that they should kill one another *reciprocally*: and there was given unto him a great *knife*." With this retranslation, does "terrorism" come to mind by any chance?

Terrorism is a form of violence that is often executed discreetly within a region. It leaves significant impact in the victimized region, as it is usually a sudden attack. The act of terrorism can breach the national security, and it is not an outright war against a foreign country. The terrorists may disguise themselves as innocent civilians, even hide amongst the victims, and the search for the wanted terrorist usually starts after the terrorist act has been completed.

If terrorism is what the verse is referring to, such a historical incident must have occurred between the seventh and ninth centuries. As discussed earlier, a major incident that occurred in the seventh century was the rise of Islam in the Middle East. The Islamic prophet Muhammad unified Arabia under Islamic religion and continued to largely expand his "Muslim conquests" from early seventh century, far to the east, to the borders of China and India, and to the west in North Africa and Iberian Peninsula. The Muslim conquests were driven by an Arabian tribal practice called *ghazw*, which was raiding activities in the local areas to collect booty from caravans or tribes who were not closely related. By altering the target and purpose of *ghazw* to a broader scope of application, what was originally a local practice later evolved into international Arab conquests.[13]

The tribal *ghazw* practice continued in different forms since the time when Arabian Peninsula was united as a state for the first time. Together with jihad, which was supported in the text of monotheistic Islam propagated by Muhammad, the tribal *ghazw* practice paved the way for effective Islamic conquest in societies such as Syria and Iraq, which were rich but weakened then.[14]

A varied form of *ghazw* practice was used to finance the Arab conquests. As Islam expanded into other regions, the Arab nomads posed pressure and threat to the residents in the sedentary areas such as Syria, Palestine, and Egypt by demanding annual tribute or lump sum payments in exchange for exclusion from their molestation. Such payment required of non-nomadic residents for protection, called *khuwwah*, became a common practice along the peripheral parts of the Middle Eastern deserts.[15]

The old tribal practice of *khuwwah* further developed into a poll tax system collected from non-Muslims. In sum, the tribal looting practice of *ghazw* spread to wider regions as *khuwwah*, which evolved into *jizyah* in Muhammad's Islam. *Jizyah* became a good source of income for Muslims who were devoted to spreading their new Islamic religion through violence. The *jizyah* tax was based on *dhimmah* (protection) laws that entitled the non-Muslims to the protection, so long as the contractually agreed amounts were paid.[16]

This *jizyah* practice of levying taxes on non-Muslims is enforced to this day to finance terrorism. As a *Forbes* article reveals in an article titled, *Islamic State Warns Christians: Convert, Pay Tax, Leave Or Die,* Muslims are financing their own terrorism by forcing non-Muslims to pay *jizyah* tax.[17]

JIHAD AND TERRORISM

The Five Pillars of Islam, also known as "the five foundations of Islam," constitute the five basic acts of Islam that serve as guiding principles of Muslims' lives. The first is Shahadah, and it refers to acknowledging that there is no other deity but Allah. Second is Salat, or the observance of obligatory ritual prayer. Third is Zakat, which is giving legal alms once a year. The fourth is Saum which is fasting during the month of Ramadan. Lastly, Haji refers to once in a lifetime pilgrimage to Mecca.[18]

What is interesting is that jihad is generally called the Sixth Pillar of Islam. This shows how significant jihad is to Muslims. Today, the Islamic word "jihad" often conjures terrorism in people's mind but its original meaning is "to strive." It does not mean to strive only, but "to strive in the path or cause of Allah."[19]

The word *jihad* is defined by the *Dictionary of Islam* as: "A religious war with those who are unbelievers in the mission of Muhammad . . . It is an incumbent religious duty, established in the Qur'an and in the Traditions as a divine institution, and enjoined specially for the purpose of advancing Islam and of repelling evil from Muslims."[20]

Jihad is classified into two kinds in general—the inner and the outer. The "inner jihad" is also called "greater jihad," as it is the inner spiritual effort. The "outer jihad" is called "lesser jihad," and it is outer physical struggle against the infidels. The "inner jihad" refers to the Muslims striving against one's own lusts in daily life in order to fulfill their religious duties in living out their beliefs. The "outer jihad" refers to the warfare against the enemies of Islam.[21]

Jihad is a word that was used from the time of Muhammad, which he regarded with high importance. For Muhammad, the primary importance was to hold "belief in Allah," and "jihad" held the second importance. The following example shows how Muhammad applied "inner jihad" in life as found in the Hadith, the collections of Muhammad's teachings, deeds, and sayings: "A man went to Muhammad, expressing a desire to join in a military jihad. The prophet asked him, 'Are your parents still living?' When the man answered in the affirmative, Muhammad told him, 'Then perform your jihad by serving and caring for them.'"[22] However, terrorists today are inclined to apply "outer jihad" more often.

Concerning the concept of jihad, there is a disparity between the Muslim and Western views. In the former, inner jihad is regarded as the essential "jihad" rather than carrying out "holy war" in fulfillment of the outer, or lesser, jihad. However, Western scholars suggest that the outer jihad was formed before the inner, and remained as the main jihad. Historically, many wars fought by Muhammad and caliphs who followed were motivated by the zeal to spread Islam and to gain financial advantages.[23]

It is said that the word "jihad" appears in the Qur'an forty-one times to generally denote wars fought "on behalf of Allah." Even though Muslims regard jihad as "holy war" for their religion, the expression "holy war" does not appear in the Qur'an even once.[24]

Jihadists, also known as the holy warriors or Mujahideen, are those who engage in jihad. Regarding the Jihadists who take part in war, the Qur'an writes:[25]

So let those fight in the cause of Allah who sell the life of this world for the Hereafter. And he who fights in the cause of Allah and is killed or achieves victory - We will bestow upon him a great reward (4:74).

It also writes:[26]

Not equal are those believers remaining [at home] - other than the disabled - and the mujahideen, [who strive and fight] in the cause of Allah with their wealth and their lives. Allah has preferred the mujahideen through their wealth and their lives over those who remain [behind], by degrees. And to both Allah has promised the best [reward]. But Allah has preferred the mujahideen over those who remain [behind] with a great reward (4:95).

Martyrdom to Muslims holds special regard, as the word "martyr" means "witness." In other words, a jihadist literally witnesses his belief by dying in the fight for Allah.[27]

With regard to this matter, the Qur'an writes:

So when you meet those who disbelieve [in battle], strike [their] necks until, when you have inflicted slaughter upon them, then secure their bonds, . . . And those who are killed in the cause of Allah - never will He waste their deeds (47:4).

Because jihadists yearn for better afterlife, they wish to witness their faith through martyrdom. This is why the perception of death in the mind of Muslim jihadists and non-Muslims are strikingly different. How death is perceived by jihadists is revealed in following passage found in the Qur'an:[28]

And never think of those who have been killed in the cause of Allah as dead. Rather, they are alive with their Lord, receiving provision, Rejoicing in what Allah has bestowed upon them of His bounty, and they receive good tidings about those [to be martyred] after them who have not yet joined them - that there will be no fear concerning them, nor will they grieve (3:169-170).

According to the Qur'an, martyrs are promised rewards:[29]

Those are the ones brought near [to Allah] in the Gardens of Pleasure, a [large] company of the former peoples and a few of the later peoples, on thrones woven [with ornament], reclining on them, facing each other. With vessels, pitchers and a cup [of wine] from a flowing spring - no headache will they have therefrom, nor will they be intoxicated - and fruit of what they select and the meat of fowl, from whatever they desire. And [for them are] fair women with large, [beautiful] eyes, the likenesses of pearls well-protected, as reward for what they used to do (56:11-24).

Contrary to a view that Islam is a religion of peace, the teachings of the Qur'an promote fighting against unbelievers.[30] For example, the Qur'an states:

Fight those who do not believe in Allah or in the Last Day and who do not consider unlawful what Allah and His Messenger have made unlawful and who do not adopt the religion of truth from those who were given the Scripture - [fight] until they give the jizyah willingly while they are humbled (9:29).

It also notes:[31] "So do not obey the disbelievers, and strive against them with the Qur'an a great striving (25:52)."

Despite the Muslim statement that jihad is really referring to inner jihad, outer jihad has been practiced with much significance given to the actual carrying out of "holy war." This act of outer jihad was actually encouraged by the Qur'an with promises of rewards and recognition of martyrdom as an act of witnessing to one's faith. Outer jihad was originally practiced in the vicinity of its birth place against local enemies, but over time its target population broadened globally.[32]

This shows that the second seal can refer to the outer jihad, a form of terrorism, carried out on a local or regional level. In fact, in modern days it has become a common practice for jihadists to inflict terror on people with different beliefs and extend their acts of terror beyond their nations' boundaries. As terror mostly takes place in situations difficult to distinguish or separate allies from enemies, in the earlier days when the outer jihad was executed within local territories, jihadists were inflicting their neighbors. Today, global terrorists act discreetly until completion of the mission. Throughout these eras, peace and security have been breached. For such reasons, the outer jihad, or terrorism, is precisely what the Scripture in Revelation is describing with regard to the second seal.

DOCTRINE OF JIHAD

In the year 750, Abbasid Caliphate, third of the Islamic caliphates, arose. Since then, scholars actively studied the achievements of Islam, noting the numerous amendments that were made after death of Muhammad. *Siyar*, the "conduct of [Islamic] state in relations to other communities," refers to Islamic International Law. Early scholars connected *siyar* only to law of war such as jihad, "campaigns, spoil, apostasy, and safe conduct."[33]

Towards the end of the eighth century, Muhammad ibn al-Ḥasan al-Shaybānī (749–805), the father of Muslim international law, wrote *Introduction to the Law of Nations,* in which he dealt with the general rules and principles governing Islam's foreign relations.[34]

The treatise dealt with classical international laws, such as "the law of treaties, the treatment of diplomats, hostages, asylum, prisoners of war, conduct on the battlefield, protection of women and children and non-combatants, contracts across the line of battle, the use of poisonous weapons, and devastation of enemy territory."[35]

In Shaybānī's work, however, jihad was not an unconditional aggressive action towards unbelievers outside the time of war. The unbelief in Islam was not a sufficient reason to wage an outer jihad against them. Early jurists' stance was that outer jihad should take place only when conflict breaks out between Muslim and unbelieving forces. In other words, the early legislation did not condone the use of outer jihad in the time of peace between Islamic and non-Islamic countries.[36]

But the change came with Abū ʿAbdullāh Muḥammad ibn Idrīs al-Shāfiʿī (767–820), who first established the doctrine that war should take place not only when unbelievers are in conflict with Islam, but for the very reason that they are unbelievers. Since then, jihad became a collective duty and Muslims had to kill whenever and wherever they found unbelievers.[37] Such doctrine was founded on the Qur'an as in the following:

> And when the sacred months have passed, then kill the polytheists wherever you find them and capture them and besiege them and sit in wait for them at every place of ambush . . . (9:5).

This doctrine of jihad against unbelievers on the basis of their infidelity alone is very aggressive. It is strikingly different from the idea of jihad being against unbelievers on the basis of their hostility against Muslims. The latter was for defending Islam, while the former was for offending infidels.

Therefore, if the doctrine of al-Shāfiʿī is followed, terrorism of killing those living in the vicinities solely on the basis that they have a different belief becomes justified. This very doctrine of al-Shāfiʿī provides legal grounds to the terrorists practicing terror in belief that their action is right. This legal principle of al-Shāfiʿī was established throughout the end of the eighth century and the beginning of the ninth century, and caused much dispute among jurists.[38]

As the Islamic empire started to decline in the tenth century, its power to eradicate non-Muslim forces dwindled, which resulted in modification of the principle established by Abū ʿAbdullāh Muḥammad ibn Idrīs al-Shāfiʿī.[39]

Nevertheless, he is appraised as having contributed the most to establishing the basic theories of Sharia, the Islamic legal system provided in the Qur'an and the Hadith. He is recognized as the first Muslim who clearly documented his legal theory. He has been highly esteemed as the "father of Muslim jurisprudence" and the "founder of the science of legal theory" since his time in the Muslim world.[40]

Theories that followed after his work elaborated or even modified the themes he dealt with in his treatise, but the origination of the legal theory is attributed to his work. An Arab medieval dictum, "Shāfiʿī is to Uṣūl al-fiqh [Principles of Islamic jurisprudence] what Aristotle was to logic," has not expired to this day ever since it has been created.[41]

In Islamic legal theory, the law is regarded as divine. Law of nature is permanent and does not change. For example, when a ball drops, it falls to the ground due to gravity. As this follows the law of nature, this phenomenon does not differ, regardless of location, time, and era. Likewise, Muslims believe that Islamic law is perfect, permanent, and applicable to every human.[42]

To Muslims, ideal life is achieved through complete adherence to this law, which comes from the Qur'an.[43] Therefore, as long as the Qur'an says, "kill the polytheists wherever you find them" (9:5), there will always be a group of Muslims who adheres to the Islamic law that justifies such action.

Today such terrorist groups are actively carrying out their beliefs, with no reason to hesitate, eradicating so-called infidels in order to establish an Islamic empire on the earth through their holy war. These groups include al-Qaeda, Hamas, Hezbollah, Islamic State, and others.

The jihadists' belief, that violence must be inflicted upon infidels, has developed into the ideology of jihadism. Those who follow this ideology have constantly been making efforts to build a world of their Muslim god on earth, utilizing any possible method. They carry out guerilla wars as well as international terrorism.

Indeed, the second seal is a great sword that took away peace from the earth through means of terror, the powerful (μέγας, *megas*; powerfully affecting) knife with which people kill each other beyond their regional as well as national boundaries.

A caliphate, or "Islamic empire," is a system of Islamic government that represents the political unity of Muslims. The first caliphate was the Rashidun Caliphate from year 632 to 661. Establishing a caliphate is the goal of Muslim Brotherhood and Islamic State, so that their religious leader becomes the political leader in the Islamic government system.

Through the incidents such as the Jasmine Revolution in Tunisia (2010) and the Arab Spring that began in Libya, Egypt, Yemen, and so on, they have been taking steps in aspiration of establishing a caliphate. The documentation of jihad served as the basis for removing the peace from the land bordering Muslim societies.

The Ottoman Empire, which existed from 1299 to 1923, also claimed the caliphate system in 1517, which was eventually abolished in 1924. In the year of 2014, Islamic State of Iraq and Levant declared itself a caliphate, although it is not recognized by any country. Muslims are eager to revive the glory of previous caliphate, and some groups do not hesitate to utilize terrorism as means to achieve their goals.

Surely, the second seal prophesied the establishment of the legal theory on jihad, which provided the basis for Muslim terrorism, around the end of the eighth century or the beginning of the ninth century.

A significant understanding can be obtained from the following article published on *Forbes* on July 19, 2014:

> IS (Islamic State) moved into Mosul [of Iraq] last month and made no secret of their plans to impose the tax. Yesterday, after Christian leaders didn't attend a meeting called by IS leaders, IS moved on those plans, issuing a formal statement. The text of the statement was simple: "We offer them three choices: Islam; the *dhimma* contract – involving payment of *Jizya;* if they refuse this they will have nothing but the sword". . . . As an organization, IS doesn't have a monopoly on the modern *jizya.* The Muslim Brotherhood forced Christian Copts in the Dalga village in Egypt to pay a *jizya* tax last year. The value was imposed inconsistently as some were forced to pay 200 Egyptian pounds per day, while others paid 500 Egyptian pounds per day; it's worth noting that no specific value for the *jizya* is mentioned in Qur'an. Those who could not pay it were attacked or forced to leave.[44]

In summary, the interpretation of the second seal would be the birth of terrorism ensued from the legalization of jihad of Islamic doctrines. Terrorism or jihad was first established by Islamic caliphates and has continued to be the defining characteristic of extreme Islam that shaped the world today.

The second seal had to occur after the year 534 when the first seal occurred, and before the tenth century when the third seal occurred. From this fact, the second seal should have occurred approximately between seventh and ninth centuries. After the rise of Muhammad, jihad was legitimized and established between the end of the eighth century and the beginning of the ninth century.

The timing of the legal establishment of jihad seems to coincide perfectly with the timing of opening of the second seal while aligning seamlessly in relation to timing of other events in Revelation. These facts suggest the legitimacy of the interpretation of the second seal.

CHAPTER 8

THE FIFTH SEAL:
SLAIN FOR THE WORD OF GOD

WHO ARE THE SOULS UNDER THE ALTAR?

To interpret the fifth seal, the pertinent Scripture first has to be well understood. The Scripture is as follows:

[Rev 6:9] And when he had opened the fifth seal, I saw under the altar the souls of them that were slain for the word of God, and for the testimony which they held:

[Rev 6:10] And they cried with a loud voice, saying, How long, O Lord, holy and true, dost thou not judge and avenge our blood on them that dwell on the earth?

[Rev 6:11] And white robes were given unto every one of them; and it was said unto them, that they should rest yet for a little season, until their fellowservants also and their brethren, that should be killed as they were, should be fulfilled.

According to the Scriptures, after the fifth seal is opened, there are souls under the altar crying out to God for their revenge. They are told to wait, because their fellow servants and brothers need to be killed also as they had been. The identification of these souls in the fifth seal can be aided by comparing them with the souls appearing in Revelation chapter 7:

[Rev 7:9] After this I beheld, and, lo, a great multitude, which no man could number, of all nations, and kindreds, and people, and tongues, stood before the throne, and before the Lamb, clothed with white robes, and palms in their hands;

In this verse, a great multitude standing before the throne are clothed with white robes. In contrast, the souls of the fifth seal are initially seen not yet clothed with white robes. Furthermore, they are described merely as "slain for the word of God, and for the testimony which they held." Is there anything different in this description from the multitude in Revelation 7? There is no mention of the Lamb, Lord Jesus Christ in the fifth seal!

More groups of souls appearing before the throne in heaven are reviewed for comparison in the following Scriptures:

[Rev 7:14] And I said unto him, Sir, thou knowest. And he said to me, These are they which came out of great tribulation, and have washed their robes, and made them white in the blood of the *Lamb*.

[Rev 14:1] And I looked, and, lo, a *Lamb* stood on the mount Sion, and with him an hundred forty and four thousand, having his Father's name written in their foreheads.

[Rev 14:4] These are they which were not defiled with women; for they are virgins. These are they which follow the *Lamb* whithersoever he goeth. These were redeemed from among men, being the firstfruits unto God and to the *Lamb*.

[Rev 15:3] And they sing the song of Moses the servant of God, and the song of the *Lamb*, saying, Great and marvellous are thy works, Lord God Almighty; just and true are thy ways, thou King of saints.

[Rev 20:4] And I saw thrones, and they sat upon them, and judgment was given unto them: and I saw the souls of them that were beheaded for the witness of *Jesus*, and for the word of God, and which had not worshipped the beast, neither his image, neither had received his mark upon their foreheads, or in their hands; and they lived and reigned with Christ a thousand years.

With all of the groups that are presented in Revelation chapters 7, 14, 15, and 20, the Lamb or Jesus is mentioned. This is in stark contrast with the souls in Revelation chapter 6, which describes the opening of the fifth seal. Could this difference be a characteristic of the souls crucial for their identification?

One of the descriptions of these souls in the fifth seal is "the souls of them that were slain." According to this description, they are people who had already died. In addition to the fact that they are dead, the description that they held their belief and/or testimony in God's Word is another common trait shared with the groups in Revelation chapters 7, 14, 15, and 20. Yet, the fact that these souls receive their white robes only now in Revelation chapter 6 is a clear difference from those in Revelation chapter 7. What, then, does this difference indicate?

Revelation 7:14 defines what the "white robe" is. The verse writes, "washed their robes, and made them white in the blood of the Lamb." This is a statement that the blood of Jesus Christ washes and makes robes white. This suggests that the robes indicate the righteousness through faith, and that those who are saved are identified with their white robes.

This definition of "white robe" clearly explains the link between the white robes and the presence of the Lamb in the Scripture. But there is no mention of the Lamb related to the robe in Revelation 6:9–11, although the souls in the fifth seal were killed for the word of God and their testimony. Let us ask, then, why were the souls under the altar in the fifth seal not already clothed with the white robes despite their martyrdom? It is absolute that a soul can be saved and become righteous only by the shedding of blood of Jesus Christ and His resurrection. Hence, the white robes definitively symbolize God's righteousness through faith in Jesus Christ. Thence, the question boils down to: Do the souls under the altar in the fifth seal, who had to wait until the time of Revelation chapter 6 to receive white robes, represent those from the Old Testament age before Jesus Christ died and rose to ascend to heaven?

The souls in the fifth seal were slain for their belief and testimony in God's word. Clearly, they are believers in God, but did not receive their white robes yet. As they had to wait for their white robes until after Jesus' crucifixion and resurrection, the Scripture of the fifth seal is indicating that these souls are from the Old Testament era and had died for the word of God before the blood of Jesus Christ was shed. Only after the Lamb shed the blood and made atonement for the sins of many, God clothed the Old Testament saints with His righteousness.

Now that the souls under the altar have been identified as the saints from the Old Testament era, the fact that they ask God to judge and avenge for them in Revelation 6:10 becomes understandable. It is precisely because they are from the Old Testament era that they say such prayers. If they were the saints from the New Testament era, they would not say such prayers, as Jesus commands the disciples in the New Testament to love their enemies and pray for those who persecute them (Mt 5:44). Surely, despite going through severe persecution, the saints in the New Testament era would hold the principle of love for enemies. Thus, the plea for vengeance in Revelation 6:10 must have been made by the saints of the Old Testament era, not the New Testament era.

In summary, the souls under the altar praying that God would avenge their blood are the saints from the Old Testament era, who are now given the white robes—the righteousness of God that comes through faith in Jesus Christ. Now that the souls of the fifth seal have been identified, the next question has to be answered: Why did God show this scene of the saints from the Old Testament era to John the apostle at the fifth seal?

THE EUROPEAN WARS OF RELIGION

When the saints from the Old Testament era ask for vengeance from God, they are told in verse 11, after they receive their white robes, to wait until another group of saints are also martyred. The fact that this occurs during the New Testament era indicates that their "fellowservants" and "brethren" in the fifth seal are Christians who are killed for their faith in Jesus during the New Testament age. In other words, the fifth seal is about the martyrdom of saints.

According to this interpretation, in the New Testament era, there must be a period of time during which many Christians were persecuted, tortured, and martyred. Of course, martyrdom and persecution have always existed throughout history. However, there may have been a certain period of time in human history during which the greatest number of Christians was martyred or killed. This historical martyrdom must have occurred after the period of time during which the fourth seal happened, which is between 1206 and 1354. Thus, the fifth seal must have been opened after 1354.

Looking back in history, this period could be traced back to the years circa 1524 to 1651 during the Protestant Reformation and Counter-Reformation by the Catholics, when many religious and/or political wars were fought across Europe. During this period, Catholics, Protestants, and Anabaptists stood opposed to each other's beliefs. Religious dissent among leaders inevitably led to political conflicts, resulting in wars and loss of many lives.

Many wars followed the Protestant Reformation, when Protestants, under the leadership of Martin Luther and others, broke away from the Roman Catholic Church. Table 8-1 lists some European wars from 1524 to 1651 connected to the Protestant Reformation. Even the lowest estimate shows an alarming death toll of brothers and sisters in Christ who died during the European wars of religion. There are still many more wars that are not included in Table 8-1 for the sake of simplicity.

In 1517, Martin Luther criticized the doctrines and practices of the Roman Catholic Church through his work,

WAR	BEGIN YEAR	END YEAR	LOWEST ESTIMATE	HIGHEST ESTIMATE
German Peasants' War	1524	1525	100,000	100,000
Battle of Kappel in Switzerland	1531	1531	-	-
Schmalkaldic War	1546	1547	-	-
Eighty Years' War	1568	1648	230,000	2,000,000
French Wars of Religion	1562	1598	2,000,000	4,000,000
Thirty Years' War	1618	1648	3,000,000	11,500,000
Wars of the Three Kingdoms	1639	1651	315,000	735,000
The European Wars of Religion (Total)	1524	1651	Total 5,645,000	Total 18,335,000

Table 8-1. European wars of religion from 1524 to 1651 that followed the Protestant Reformation.[1, 2, 3, 4] Lowest and highest estimates of death tolls are provided, with the sum total in the last row.

The Ninety-Five Theses. This led to excommunication of Luther from the Catholic Church in 1521, and was the beginning of the Protestant Reformation.[5] Luther was joined by other reformers, such as Ulrich Zwingli and John Calvin. Different denominations within Protestantism were formed from each of the major reformers. The theological disputes and conflicts started in Germany and then gradually spread throughout Europe, including England.

Aside from religious conflicts, the Reformation movement also brewed political conflicts. So, in response to the Protestant Reformation, the Roman Catholic Church incited the Counter-Reformation. Until the wars ended, European countries underwent vast changes in religio-political landscape.

The German Peasants' War occurred from 1524 to 1525 in modern-day Germany, Switzerland, Austria, and other regions of central Europe where German was spoken. Although religious conflicts were not a direct cause, it is known that Luther's religious revolution added heat to the conflicts that led to peasants' revolt against authorities.[6, 7]

In 1531, the Battle of Kappel was fought between Protestants and Catholics in Switzerland. This battle led to the death of Zwingli.[8] The Schmalkaldic War was fought in the Holy Roman Empire from 1546 to 1547, between the Holy Roman Emperor Charles V and his imperial forces against the Schmalkaldic League established by Lutheran leaders and princes.[9]

The Eighty Years' War, 1568 to 1648, also called the Dutch War of Independence, was partly caused by Protestants, primarily by Calvinists, fighting for religious freedom against Roman Catholic repression led by Philip II of Spain, who reigned over Netherlands.[10]

The French Wars of Religion represent a period of time from 1562 to 1598, during which civil wars were fought between Catholics and Protestants, especially Calvinists. An alternative view exists on the period of the war that it occurred from 1562 to 1629.[11] The Wars of the Three Kingdoms, which is also known as the English Revolution, happened among three kingdoms of Scotland, England, and Ireland between 1639 and 1651.[12]

The Thirty Years' War, which occurred from 1618 to 1648, is considered one of the most destructive conflicts in the history of Europe. As can be seen in Table 8-1, this war has the highest estimated death tolls among the mentioned European Wars of Religion. It started out with religious conflicts between Protestants and Catholics in the Holy Roman Empire, where today's Germany is located. Over time, political conflicts also arose between political powers of different religious backgrounds and beliefs. Conflicts existed between the Catholics and Protestants, as well as minorities such as Calvinists and Anabaptists. As a result, wars were fought not only in the Holy Roman Empire but throughout the European continent over time as well.[13]

The states that participated in the Thirty Years' War were the states of the Holy Roman Empire, Austria, Bavaria, Saxony, Palatinate, Hesse-Kassel, Brandenburg, Russia, Netherlands, Denmark, Sweden, France, England, Savoy, Transylvania, Spain, Poland, and others.[14] With almost all of Europe participating, the results of this very long war were devastating. For instance, population was reduced by a third in the Czech lands, today's Czech Republic.[15] In Germany, almost half of the male population died.[16] The following excerpt describes the state of devastation in Germany at the end of the Thirty Years' War:

> The losses of the civil population were almost incredible. In a certain district of Thuringia which was probably better off than the greater part of Germany, there were, before the war cloud burst, 1,717 houses standing in nineteen villages. In 1649, only 627 houses were left. And even of the houses which remained many were

untenanted. The 1,717 houses had been inhabited by 1,773 families. Only 316 families could be found to occupy the 627 houses. Property fared still worse. In the same district 244 oxen alone remained of 1,402. Of 4,616 sheep, not one was left. Two centuries later the losses thus suffered were scarcely recovered.[17]

What ignited the start of the Thirty Years' War had largely to do with the Peace of Augsburg, a treaty signed between the Holy Roman Emperor Charles V and the Schmalkaldic League in the year 1555. This treaty supposedly ended the religious and military struggle between the Catholics and Lutherans, but established several principles that actually failed to completely end all of the religious struggles.[18]

Under the principle *Cuius regio, eius religio*, a Latin phrase that means "Whoever has the kingdom chooses the religion," the religion of a region was determined by the ruler of that state in Germany. If the prince of a state was Catholic, the inhabitants would have to be Catholic. If the prince was Lutheran, inhabitants would have to be Lutheran.[19] Under this principle, if a Catholic prince were to convert to Lutheranism, then all residents within the prince's entire estate needed to convert to Protestantism.

Thus, another principle called *reservatum ecclesiasticum* was inserted into the treaty by imperial decree that forced princes converting to Lutheranism to forfeit their seats to Catholic princes and thereby maintaining the balance of Catholic-ruled states in the empire.[20] With these principles in effect, both Catholics and Lutherans in the German-speaking states of the Holy Roman Empire kept checks and balances on each power.

However, under the treaty, other Protestant groups such as Calvinists and Anabaptists remained unprotected and were charged with heresy. And heretics were punished by death.[21] These minor groups were not recognized nor legally protected until the Peace of Westphalia was established in the year 1648, ending the Thirty Years' War.[22] Thus, persecution and martyrdom continued to exist even after the establishment of the Peace of Augsburg in 1555.

Anabaptists were persecuted in great numbers, and their martyrs were executed in cruel, brutal ways. They were captured, imprisoned, interrogated, tortured, hung, beheaded, buried alive, pierced with forks into their bowels, burned with fire, strangled, and drowned in the sea and the river, thrown down the cliff, and pierced through with spears to the bottom of the cliff.[23]

Catholics and Protestants, including Lutherans and Calvinists, considered Anabaptists as heretics, because Anabaptists did not believe in infant baptism. Anabaptists believed that infant baptism was not effective, as baptism should be administered only to adults who are capable of professing their faith.

Persecution of Anabaptists was first led by Ulrich Zwingli, a Protestant reformer in Zurich, Switzerland, and the first Anabaptist brother martyred at Zurich was Felix Mentz, who was drowned in 1527. Countless Anabaptists were persecuted and martyred by Protestants and Catholics afterwards. In 1837, a 1,290-page book, *The Bloody Theatre, or Martyrs' Mirror, of the Defenceless Christians: Who Suffered and Were Put to Death for the Testimony of Jesus, Their Savior, from the Time of Christ until the Year A.D. 1660*, was written to document the stories of Christian martyrs. The book remarkably notes the history of Anabaptist martyrs between 1525 and 1660.[24, 25]

What makes this period of time in European history unique is that Christians victimized one another. Catholics warred against all non-Catholic faith and renounced to accept any disparate theological adherents. The martyrdom of Anabaptists prolonged until 1660, and they were persecuted for their testimony even by Protestants such as Lutherans and Calvinists.

Revelation 6:9–11 informs that the opening of the fifth seal would involve loss of many Christian brethren. The description differs from those of other prophetic events of the seals in the book of Revelation in that it specifies "who" are to die in the incident. According to the Scriptures, the victims in the fifth seal are not just any men or women, but categorically believers in Jesus Christ, as stated in verse 11, "their fellow servants also and their brethren."

Based on the history presented above about the years during the Reformation in Europe, from 1524 to 1660, that instigated innumerable deaths of Christian brethren, the prophecy of the fifth seal in Revelation 6:9–11 is deemed fulfilled during the sixteenth and seventeenth centuries.

CHAPTER 9

THE SIXTH SEAL: GREAT EARTHQUAKE

THE GREAT LISBON EARTHQUAKE

The sixth seal in the book of Revelation consists of several different events. The pertinent Scriptures are as follows:

[Rev 6:12] And I beheld when he had opened the sixth seal, and, lo, there was a great earthquake; and the sun became black as sackcloth of hair, and the moon became as blood;

[Rev 6:13] And the stars of heaven fell unto the earth, even as a fig tree casteth her untimely figs, when she is shaken of a mighty wind.

[Rev 6:14] And the heaven departed as a scroll when it is rolled together; and every mountain and island were moved out of their places.

[Rev 6:15] And the kings of the earth, and the great men, and the rich men, and the chief captains, and the mighty men, and every bondman, and every free man, hid themselves in the dens and in the rocks of the mountains;

[Rev 6:16] And said to the mountains and rocks, Fall on us, and hide us from the face of him that sitteth on the throne, and from the wrath of the Lamb:

[Rev 6:17] For the great day of his wrath is come; and who shall be able to stand?

The events in the sixth seal are a great earthquake, darkening of the sun, the moon becoming like blood, stars falling, mountains and islands moving from their places, and people hiding from and fearing God's judgment. Historical records on each of these incidents would bear undeniable testimony to the fact that the sixth seal had already been opened.

The first effect of the sixth seal is a great earthquake. Since the sixth seal must come after the fifth seal, which ended in 1660, the great earthquake must be a post-1660 incident. As will be discussed in the next volume, the first trumpet is interpreted to have been sounded in the year 1914. Based on the belief that the book of Revelation is written in the order of the events' occurrence, the seventh seal should be interpreted to have been opened before the year 1914.

The search for the "great earthquake" began with looking up a list of great earthquakes in history. The selected list of historical earthquakes with magnitude higher than 7.0 that occurred between the years of 1660 and 1914 is in Table 9-1.

DATE	LOCATION	MAGNITUDE	FATALITIES
October 3, 1914	Burdur, Turkey (Ottoman Empire)	M 7.0	4,000
August 9, 1912	Murefte, Turkey (Ottoman Empire)	M 7.8	2,800
June 15, 1911	Ryukyu Islands, Japan	M 8.1	12
January 23, 1909	Silakhor, Iran (Persia)	M 7.3	6,000
December 28, 1908	Messina, Italy	M 7.2	70,000
October 21, 1907	Qaratog, Tajikistan	M 8.0	12,000
August 17, 1906	Valparaiso, Chile	M 8.2	3,882
April 18, 1906	San Francisco, California	M 7.8	3,000
January 31, 1906	Off the Coast of Esmeraldas, Ecuador	M 8.8	1,000
April 4, 1905	Kangra, India	M 7.5	19,000
June 12, 1897	Assam, India	M 8.3	1,500
June 15, 1896	*Sanriku, Japan*	*M 8.5*	*27,000*
October 27, 1891	Mino-Owari, Japan	M 8.0	7,273
May 10, 1877	Offshore Tarapaca, Chile	M 8.3	34

May 18, 1875	Northern Colombia	M 7.3	16,000
August 13, 1868	*Arica, Peru (now Chile)*	*M 9.0*	*25,000*
April 3, 1868	Ka'u District, Island of Hawaii	M 7.9	77
December 16, 1857	Naples, Italy	M 6.9	11,000
February 8, 1843	Leeward Islands	M 8.3	5,000
July 10, 1821	Camana, Peru	M 8.2	162
February 4, 1783	Calabria, Italy	-	50,000
November 1, 1755	*Lisbon, Portugal*	*M 8.7*	*70,000*
June 7, 1755	Kashan, Iran	-	40,000
July 8, 1730	Valparaiso, Chile	M 8.7	5
January 26, 1700	Cascadia Subduction Zone	M 9.0	-
January 11, 1693	Sicily, Italy	M 7.5	60,000
November 1667	Shemakha, Caucasia	-	80,000

Table 9-1. Selected list of historical earthquakes between 1660 and 1914.[1] Earthquakes with magnitude around 9.0 and great fatalities are italicized.

There have been many earthquakes throughout history with varying magnitudes and number of fatalities. With such high frequency, the probability of identifying the exact earthquake in verse 12 could be low. Therefore, to enhance interpretational accuracy, significant earthquakes with magnitude reaching 9.0 which caused great fatalities were screened. (For reference, the great earthquake that happened in Japan on March 11, 2011 near the East Coast of Honshu was reported to have magnitude of 9.0 with fatalities of 20,352 people.)[2]

In Table 9-1, three earthquakes are identified as having magnitude of near 9.0 and causing many fatalities, so they are italicized. Earthquakes with great magnitude but insignificant fatalities and those with many fatalities but lower magnitude were not included in the starting list for analysis. Earthquakes with high fatalities but without any record available on their magnitude towards the bottom of Table 9-1 were also excluded from the starting list.

Out of the selected three, the Great Lisbon Earthquake seemed to bear the most significance, judging by the high fatalities and its geographic location. On November 1, 1755, a great earthquake occurred in Lisbon, Portugal. Lisbon is the capital and the largest city of Portugal. The earthquake is known to have destroyed 85 percent of the city of Lisbon, leaving its buildings in ruins. In fact, it is known as the greatest earthquake in European history.[3]

The earthquake was felt not only over the entire Iberian Peninsula, but also reached central Europe.[4] Back then, there was no technology to measure the magnitude of an earthquake. The magnitude of this earthquake on historical record is an estimation based on modern seismology and damage observation questionnaires collected right after the earthquake.[5] The magnitude of the Great Lisbon Earthquake is estimated to be in the range of 8.5 to 9.0 on the moment magnitude scale.[6]

The destruction caused by the Great Lisbon Earthquake was on an apocalyptic scale. The earthquake lasted for nine minutes, and fierce fire burned the city for five days. It is estimated that in Lisbon only, a total of between 10,000 and 100,000 were killed or injured from the earthquake, tsunami, and fire.[7]

Thirty minutes after the earthquake, there was a huge tsunami, both of which were totally unexpected in terms of their occurrences and magnitude.[8] A tsunami seven meters high reached one region of Lisbon, which flooded the city. The tsunami spread vastly, reaching the London harbor, Italy, Norway, North African coastlines, the Canary Islands, the Azores, and even the East coast of North America.[9]

DEBATE OVER THE CAUSE

In 1755, Lisbon was known as "one of the most beautiful cities" and "an international commerce centre" in Europe. The city was filled with wealth, palaces, and churches, and traders from various parts of the world. English and German traders were greatly involved in business in the city of Lisbon. Religiously, Lisbon was famous for the inquisition, superstition, and idolatry.[10] Having been such a prominent city, the destruction caused by the earthquake was recognized as a miserable catastrophe throughout Europe, and to European trading cities, such as London, Amsterdam, Hamburg, and Venice, as an incident of "extreme consternation" due to their large sums of investments in Lisbon.[11]

The earthquake in Lisbon greatly stirred up the communities in Europe even more because it occurred on

November 1st, All Saints' Day. Scholars suggest that if it had occurred on the previous day or the next day, it most likely would have caused less social and religious commotion throughout Europe, and it may have received less attention. All Saints' Day was "the highest catholic festival," and it had a grave importance in Lisbon since it was also a "judgment day of the inquisition." During the inquisition, the Roman Catholics judged heretics, and punished, persecuted, and sometimes even killed the people that they deemed heretic.[12]

The earthquake hit Lisbon at 9:40 in the morning. By this time, the churches were full of people attending the first Mass of All Saints' Day. Many churches were filled up to their seating capacities, and when the earthquake hit the city of Lisbon, "30 of the 40 churches collapsed," killing many inside the church buildings. Survivors ran for their lives, but were soon struck by the tsunami waves. Fire in various places caused more fatalities, resulting in a massive death toll.[13]

Far beyond Lisbon, the trembling and shaking of the earthquake was felt in Paris, England, northern Finland, Scotland, Germany, and other places of Europe. This spread of earthquake waves arrived at these places faster than the news of the earthquake in Lisbon, leaving the European societies mentally shocked, fearful, and confused.[14]

Many questioned God for allowing such a huge catastrophe to happen in Lisbon and why God would allow it to happen to His faithful followers, especially on All Saints' Day. These topics were heatedly "discussed at Lisbon and throughout Europe by philosophers, theologians, politicians and artists."[15]

Many persisted on their belief that the origin of earthquakes is divine and under the control of God. However, many new ideas also developed and insisted that earthquakes and other natural disasters are natural phenomenon, not results of God's providence.[16] The debate was so intense that it was called the "eighteenth century earthquake-theology."[17]

Catholic and Protestant believers and clergy accepted the Lisbon earthquake as God's "deliberate punishment" of people for their sins, and this point of view was preached in "sermons, tracts, and moralizing poetry" in all parts of Europe. A "Trinitarian theologian and preacher" named Agustín Sanchez wrote, "God uses the creatures to infuse fear in sinner and to move them to repentance."[18] Miguel de San José, the "Bishop of Guadix and Baza," most firmly defended the divine and supernatural character of the Lisbon earthquake. He wrote, "only to deny or doubt that earthquakes and other disasters are usually the effect of the wrath of God, can be considered as an error in the faith."[19]

The Great Lisbon Earthquake resulted in an intense discussion over its cause, and led many religious people to fear God's judgment, examine themselves to repentance, and acknowledge God's divine involvement in nature for punishment of the sinful.[20]

This debate was heated by strong opposing views throughout Europe. The opponents firmly believed that the Lisbon earthquake was nothing but a natural phenomenon. They insisted that natural disasters had no relation to divinity or superstition and sought scientific and natural explanations for the earthquake.[21]

This resulted in "the birth of modern seismology" and disaster management led by Marquês de Pombal, who was ordered to manage the emergency situations and reconstruct the city of Lisbon by King José Manuel I of Portugal. Marquês de Pombal, the "founder of seismology," ended up convicting a Jesuit preacher, Malagrida, at a trial for preaching against the natural causes of earthquakes and emphasizing repentance to God by insisting that the Lord was "still shaking the Earth."[22]

As a result, the practice of inquisition was terminated in Portugal, and Marquês de Pombal continued to rebuild the city of Lisbon, taking care of the burial of 30,000–60,000 corpses, medical services for the injured, distribution of food, taxation, and security. From this point in history, earthquakes and other disasters that were once believed as acts of divine intervention were believed to be caused by nature.[23]

The Great Earthquake of Lisbon most likely was the manifestation of the sixth seal. The timing of the incident is in line with the chronological unveiling of the seals, and it also began the onset of lasting effect as it mutated the conventional belief-system in God and the supernatural. This was the time in history that a new culture was conceived where people began to rely on science for explanation and started to deny confiding in religion for inexplicable incidents.

CHAPTER 10

THE SIXTH SEAL:
SUN BECAME BLACK, AND MOON AS BLOOD

THE SUN BECAME BLACK AS SACKCLOTH OF HAIR

The great earthquake that marks the beginning of the sixth seal is identified as the Great Lisbon Earthquake in 1755. This identification may not be fully convincing to some readers as a stand-alone interpretation. However, there are four separate events prophesied with regard to the sixth seal. If the interpretation of all four events shows that corresponding historical incidents occurred in the chronological order presented in Revelation, the interpretation of the Great Lisbon Earthquake is no longer a stand-alone interpretation. Instead, the likelihood that the "great earthquake" of the sixth seal was indeed the Great Lisbon Earthquake increases. If the identification of the Great Lisbon Earthquake is correct, then the second event of the sixth seal that follows the earthquake is expected to have happened after 1755.

To identify the second event of the sixth seal, the description in the Scripture needs to be understood first. Regarding the event, the Scripture writes, "the sun became black as sackcloth of hair, and the moon became as blood" (Rev 6:12b).

In search of this strange occurrence, the search phrase "dark day" was used. Rather unexpectedly and too handily, the discovery was immediate: "New England's Dark Day." This phenomenon occurred on May 19, 1780, which was certainly later than the Lisbon earthquake in 1755.

Remarkably, these incidents occurred in the order as they are written in Revelation. After the earthquake in Lisbon in 1755, an unusually darkened sky appeared during the daytime on May 19, 1780 and continued until the next night, throughout certain regions in New England and Canada.[1]

During "New England's Dark Day," there was darkness because the sunlight did not shine upon the affected areas. Back then, there was no method of rapid communication as in modern days. Thus, people could only determine in retrospect where the darkness had fallen by sharing their observations through letters and newspapers printed in different regions.[2] Using this method, Professor Samuel Williams of Harvard College collected information about the darkness in different states and concluded that it had been seen throughout a vast area of New England, "as far south as northern New Jersey and New York City coastal waters, as far north as Portland, Maine and west into the Hudson Valley."[3]

The following passage is from his observation of the darkness from Cambridge, which was published in *The Analytical Review, Or History of Literature, Domestic and Foreign, on an Enlarged Plan*:

This extraordinary darkness came on between the hours of 10 and 11 A.M. and continued till the middle of the next night. In most parts of the country it was so great, that people were unable to read common print, or to manage their domestic business, in the middle of the day, without candles. It extended all over the New England States, and in some directions probably much farther; the prospect bearing the gloom of night, so that the fowls everywhere retired to rest, and the birds, having sung their evening songs, disappeared and became silent. From the atmospheric phenomena which prevailed at the time, and other circumstances, it appears that this darkness was occasioned by the smoke and ashes arising from large fires, which had been made some time before, by the people in the western parts of the States of New Hampshire and Vermont, for the purpose of clearing their lands; the state of the wind being such as prevented the quick dispersion of these heavy vapours.[4]

In December of 1785, Dr. Samuel Tenney wrote a letter about the Dark Day, proposing his idea that unusually thick layers of clouds may have caused the darkness by blocking the path and thus reducing the velocities of light rays. The following passage is reproduced from his letter that was later published in the *Collections of the Massachusetts Historical Society*:

Although the uncommon darkness, which attracted the attention of all ranks of people in this part of the country, on the 19th of May, 1780, was a phenomenon which several gentlemen of considerable literary abilities have endeavoured to solve, yet I believe you will agree with me that no satisfactory solution has yet appeared… As I set out the next day, from my father's at Rowley, to join my regiment in New-Jersey, I had an opportunity to inform myself what were the appearances in different parts of the country between here and Pennsylvania. The result of my inquiries, on that journey, and after my return, was that the darkness was most gross in the county of Essex, the lower part of the state of New-Hampshire and the old Province of Maine. In Rhode-Island and Connecticut it was not so great, and still less in New-York. In New-Jersey the second stratum of clouds was observed, but not of any great thickness; nor was the darkness very uncommon. In the lower parts of Pennsylvania, if my recollection does not fail me, no extraordinary appearance was noticed. Through this whole extent the lower stratum had an uncommon brassy hue, while the earth and trees were adorned with so enchanting a verdure as could not escape notice, even amidst the unusual gloom that surrounded the spectator. This gradual increase of the darkness from southwest to northeast, which was nearly the course of the clouds, affords a pretty good argument in favour of the supposition, that they were condensed by two strong currents of wind blowing in different directions . . . The darkness of the following evening was probably as gross as ever has been observed since the Almighty fiat gave birth to light. It wanted only palpability to render it as extraordinary, as that which overspread the land of Egypt in the days of Moses. And as darkness is not substantial, but a mere privation, the palpability ascribed to that by the sacred historian must have arisen from some peculiar affection of the atmosphere, perhaps an exceeding thick vapour, that accompanied it. I could not help conceiving at the time, that if every luminous body in the universe had been shrouded in impenetrable shades, or struck out of existence, the darkness could not have been more complete. A sheet of white paper held within a few inches of the eyes was equally invisible with the blackest velvet.[5]

Such are the accounts on New England's Dark Day. The cause and origins of the darkness were unknown and still remain unknown today. As the passages above show, people enthusiastically tried to solve the mystery of the Dark Day. As such a darkening phenomenon was so uncommon, only conjecture and speculation abounded regarding its origins.

Back then, there were barely any organized scientific societies or regularly published journals devoted to scientific inquiry and discussion of the findings. Instead, the people in New England discussed various matters not only in local communities but also in the vast New England communities via newspapers, pamphlets, broadsides, letters, journals, diaries, as well as religious tracts and sermons. Such local papers shared throughout New England communities revealed ample observations of the Dark Day phenomenon that led to potential explanations as to what had caused it.[6]

In Weston, Massachusetts, a merchant and judge Samuel Phillips Savage noted a remarkably thick air and a very red sun rising and setting for several days before the Dark Day. Others accounted for a pinkish waning moon as well. According to Savage, in the morning of the Dark Day, the sky had turned into a "pale Cyder" color, tinted with "a light grassy hue." Towards ten o'clock in the morning, the sky was darkened similar to a solar eclipse, and the sun had nearly entirely gone from appearance. At the unusually early coming of darkness, birds stopped singing and domestic animals went back to their cages, and people working in kitchens, barnyards, schoolhouses, churches, workshops, sea, forests, fields, and pastures stopped working and wondered at the sky.[7]

As darkness quickly fell upon the New England region, workers and school children headed back home, and many ran to the meetinghouses for sermons in fear of the judgment day. At noon, those who fed themselves lunch did so by candlelight. People with good vision could not read from papers or clocks. Even with his spectacles on, Savage stated he had difficulty reading the time on his watch in front of a large window. His neighbor farmer could not tell the difference between the ground and manure he was spreading in his field. Although it was supposed to be daytime, the songs of night birds were heard in the darkness.[8]

In Sudbury, Massachusetts, Experience Richardson stated that in such terrible darkness, people were unable to see their own hands.[9] Savage could not rely on his vision, and could discern the windows from the walls only by feeling. He described that all he could see around him was universal blackness.[10]

Around nine o'clock in the evening, people in Boston finally saw the moon. What they observed was a nearly full moon in bloodred color, not pinkish like it had been for the last several days or silver-colored like it usually is. However, the bloodred moonlight was soon overcome by the darkness, and the terrible darkness that remained for the night and the next day was compared to the darkness that befell Egypt in the time of Moses in an account published in the *Massachusetts Spy*.[11, 12]

The darkness that came upon the New England states so suddenly with a rise of a bloodred moon at nighttime sparked perhaps the most natural response from the religious New England communities.

According to the essay, *"Mark Well the Gloom": Shedding Light on the Great Dark Day of 1780*, written by a professor and author, Thomas J. Campanella, and published in the journal *Environmental History*, "MANY—PERHAPS MOST—New Englanders responded to the sudden darkness by turning to God. All day and into the night the faithful rushed to their meetinghouses."[13]

This was a natural and expected response from the religious New Englanders. They were very familiar with the Biblical prophecies about the end times, and they regarded the sudden appearance of the black sun and the red moon as the fulfillment of the prophecies. Therefore, when they found themselves in the midst of the "preternatural darkness," they turned to God and gathered at their meetinghouses, expecting to hear the last trumpet being blown and see the end of the world.[14] In a poem about the Dark Day entitled "Abraham Davenport," John Greenleaf Whittier wrote:

*Men prayed, and women wept; all ears grew sharp
To hear the doom-blast of the trumpet shatter
The black sky, that the dreadful face of Christ
Might look from the rent clouds, not as he looked
A loving guest at Bethany, but stern
As Justice and inexorable Law.*[15]

According to a clergyman-diarist Timothy Dwight, most people believed that the judgment day was imminent. Reverend David Hall wrote in his journal that the crowd of people gathered at the meetinghouse for prayer and requested his presence for his leadership.[16]

Throughout and even after the Dark Day, the sound of the trumpet that everyone so expected to hear was not heard. This, however, did not discourage the discussion of the Dark Day in relation to the end of the world afterwards. After the Dark Day, many tracts and sermons explaining the occurrence of the Dark Day in light of the end time prophecy in the Bible were published. For example, a deacon of the Second Congregational Church in Marblehead, Massachusetts named Samuel Gatchel delved into the Bible and analyzed various passages in order to "discern the Signs of the Times" (Mt 16:3).[17]

Many humbly perceived the darkness that prevailed in New England as a sign from God, alert about the end of the world. In fact, the mindset of many New Englanders was stoic and strictly focused on religious virtues. Even the politicians and authorities in legislature were religious and sought to be found faithful before God.[18]

In Connecticut, Senator Abraham Davenport became famous for continuing to work in the midst of the Dark Day, even when his fellow lawmakers pleaded with him to adjourn their duties. He answered them by declaring, "The day of judgment is either approaching, or it is not. If it is not, there is no cause of an adjournment: if it is, I choose to be found doing my duty. I wish therefore that candles may be brought."[19]

With the accounts about the Dark Day in various forms of writings—letters, news articles, broadsides, sermons, pamphlets, tracts, poems, diaries, and journals as well as folklore, this unusual and historically unique incident has been well recorded. Over time, the information gathered about the incident was used to speculate as to the cause of the darkness. While many focused on the religious and prophetic explanation of the incident, many philosophers and scientists also focused on gathering data from various written accounts and empirical data from the fields to explain the occurrence of such darkness.[20]

To some Christians, this act of scientific investigation to seek answers beyond Biblical explanation was deemed heretical, while other Christians saw perfect coherence between the laws of nature and its obedience to God, the Creator of all things. Either way, the local papers published in New England communities served as a medium for scientific debate and encouraged, even implored, people to submit their exact accounts on the Dark Day phenomenon as well as their theories on the causes of the preternatural darkness.[21]

As a consequence of the active debate forum provided in the papers, readers had access to many different theories about the darkness. One writer from Paxton, Massachusetts, Samuel Sterns, explained that one of his neighbors believed that the darkness was due to a "blazing star" that came between the earth and the sun, and another believed that the star was either Venus or Mercury passing by, while some suggested a presence of a great mountain that was blocking the sunlight but took its leave as the Dark Day phenomenon ended.[22]

Sterns himself theorized that due to the strong sunlight hitting the atmosphere of the earth for several days before the darkness impended, various particles composing the waters, volcanic fumes, and juice of plants were heated enough to ascend into the sky, then accumulate over time in the air to form a dense layer, eventually blocking the light from the sun and the moon.[23]

Another writer, "Viator" from Ipswich, Massachusetts demonstrated that he and his friends noticed smoke and vapor in the sky which obscured the atmosphere for several days before the Dark Day. He also explained that the sun and the moon had also "appeared unusually red." On May 19, they observed a red sun before the darkness came, and about nine o'clock in the morning it started to rain. Because of the thick clouds in the sky, they expected a great storm, but they only experienced small amount of wind and rain. Around three o'clock in the afternoon, when they carefully walked outside, they immediately "'perceived a strong *sooty* smell.'"[24]

Some thought that the smell originated from a burning chimney, but some suggested that the smell originated from burnt leaves. When Viator observed the rain collected in tubs in his neighborhood, he found scum consisting of black ashes and burnt leaves floating in the water, which smelled strongly of the same soot he smelled in the air. Thus, he concluded that smoke and burnt leaves were floating in the air, which obscured the sunlight as well as moonlight for several days and now were brought down with the rainfall.[25]

He theorized: "The vast body of smoke from the woods which had been burning for many days, mixing with the common exhalations from the earth and water, and condensed by the action of winds from opposite points, may perhaps be sufficient causes to produce the surprising darkness."[26]

What Viator theorized was very close to the currently most accepted theory about the cause of the darkness. Other philosophers and scientists theorized that several layers of thick, dense clouds moving in the course of the wind blocked the sunlight from reaching the affected region.[27]

Many accounted that since several days before the Dark Day, the sky had been filled with smoke, the air smelled like burning leaves, and birds dropped dead, scattered on the ground, probably due to suffocating from abundant smoke in the air. A horse-riding man could not breathe well in the woods because of thick smoke, and another had observed dark "scum like soot" on the surface of a river. People could not use the rain water they collected to wash because the water was too black. After the Dark Day had passed, some observed dark soot all over a region where the snow-covered ground had been raked and cleaned of wood chips and dirt beforehand.[28]

There were theories about the earth "passing through the tail of a comet," but these were rejected as the sun and stars would still be visible in the presence of the tails. They were disputed with further arguments that there were no differences in the tides observed on the Dark Day, which were expected to rise if there was a comet near Earth.[29]

A much more popular theory of solar eclipse was also disputed, as ever since ancient civilization solar eclipses have been predicted and easily recognizable. Also, solar eclipses are observed only for a few minutes, as the moon quickly moves away from the solar ecliptic location. Thus, the darkness that lasted for more than a day on May 19, 1780 couldn't possibly have been caused by a solar eclipse.[30]

In fact, according to NASA, there were two solar eclipses that occurred in the year 1780, an annular solar eclipse on the fourth of May and a total solar eclipse on the twenty-seventh of October.[31] Both did not occur any time close enough to impact the darkness on May 19.

The astronomical theories about the Dark Day phenomenon were therefore refuted, and theories that suggested presence of substance in the air blocking the sun and the moon lights in New England were deemed more probable. One such theory was volcanic fumes obstructing the sun and the moon from view. However, there were no volcanic eruptions nearby around the nineteenth of May. In fact, on May 18, a day before the Dark Day, there was a second eruption of Mount Etna in Italy, following the first eruption in April, but this volcano was located too far away to cause such an intense darkness specifically over New England for a day and a half.[32]

Today, the primary cause of the Dark Day phenomenon is believed to be what Viator had theorized. The most accepted theory about the darkness is that a combination of various elements—smoke, soot, and ashes of burnt leaves from forest fires, and rise of vapors and atmospheric dust from the massive amount of snow melting after an especially long, icy winter—formed layers of thick fog and cloud in the sky, blocking the rays of the sun and the moon during the Dark Day.[33]

Viator's theory is primarily accepted as the explanation of the darkness on the Dark Day, as it is supported with records of certain environmental factors of New England in May, 1780. During this time, an unusually prolonged and extensive burning of forests in preparation for cultivation was done, which resulted in massive amount of smoke, ashes, and burnt leaves filling the surrounding atmosphere. The fact that such activities were ongoing right before the Dark Day occurred is most likely not a coincidence. A weekly newspaper, *Independent Chronicle*, reported on June 6, 1780 an account of forest fires witnessed by three men from Haverhill. The following is an excerpt from the published account:

> Have also seen three gentlemen who left Haverhill, on Connecticut River, the same day . . . They say the morning was cloudy; there was a little rain, with thunder. As they travelled on, they observed to one another, it was uncommonly dark: About 12 o'clock, so dark they could not see a man more than 20 rods. These gentlemen say, the woods in these parts, and as far as Ticonderoga, had been burning for some time with

amazing fury. The fires were raging to such a degree, in several townships through which they passed, that they were in danger of being suffocated. I am informed, that in the Cohass the fires raged to such a degree, that great damage has been done to the timber; some houses, mills, bridges, and a vast deal of fence, have been consumed. Those gentlemen say, as they came down the country, whenever they were upon a high piece of ground, which gave them a prospect, the woods on all quarters appeared to be on fire . . . He further observes, the air was uncommonly thick, and afforded an unusual smell. Between nine and ten at night, he ordered his men to take in some of the sails, but it was so dark they could not find the way from one mall to the other . . . The gentleman of New Hampshire, whose letter was published in the Independent Ledger, last Monday, mentions the soot, or ashes, which appeared . . . on the river,–which rendered the rain water unfit for use, and covered a snow-drift all over. Many other accounts of the same kind have been mentioned by gentlemen of observation. I remember burnt pieces of leaves have been seen falling on Cambridge common, and also in the streets of Boston, after large fires back in the country. I am fully satisfied the darkness was occasioned by vast exhalations which were made for several warm days before, together with the smoke of burning woods . . . Vast tracts of woods, when the pines and leaves are dry, burning with amazing fury, must afford smoke sufficient to be a very considerable cause of darkness.[34]

As this and many other accounts report, there were huge forest fires that had been started throughout vast communities of New England for the purposes of cultivating the land for agriculture. Such burning of forest was customary for Native Americans, and New Englanders also used the method to clear out the land for cultivation. Fires started for this purpose, as well as for expansion of settlement, was observed all throughout New England—"New Hampshire, Vermont, Maine, and parts of southern Canada and eastern New York in the weeks prior to May 19."[35]

According to Professor Samuel Williams, the degree to which forests were put on fire in the spring of 1780 was much greater than usual, which caused some fires to continue to burn the woods for several days.[36] Thus, there is sufficient evidence that there were extensive fires burning down vast areas of wood in New England, causing soot and ashes to fill the air in significant amount and concentration. There were smell of burnt leaves everywhere and ashes found in rivers and basins and on earth. As smell of soot was observed during the Dark Day, the forest fires would be one of the reasons the great darkness befell on the Dark Day.

Another environmental cause of the Dark Day is believed to be the winters between 1450 and 1850 called the Little Ice Age. During this time, bitter coldness persisted during the winters throughout Europe and North America.[37] In New England, the winter preceding the Dark Day in 1780 was an especially bitter one, as it is recorded as one of the harshest and coldest winters in the history of America. For the month of January, 1780, the average temperature in the city of Hartford, Connecticut, was 4 degrees Fahrenheit, or about -16 degrees Celsius.[38] The winter of 1780 was so severe that during a ten days period, four heavy snowstorms swept through New England, leaving all the ports along the East Coast frozen.[39]

According to the accounts about the winter of 1780, snowstorms came one after another throughout the winter, depriving New Englanders of fuel so that many even had to forgo their apple trees to stay warm at home. One account reported that the height of snow was about seven feet at one point in January due to persistent, heavy snowfall.[40]

Due to such long winter full of snowfalls, the surface of the earth in New England had been frozen for months. In May, the earth was still frozen, and one could find places covered with snow in New England in early May of 1780. For two weeks before the Dark Day, however, an "unseasonably mild" weather melted the coldness away in New England. The warm air meeting the surface of the earth that had stayed cold for months most likely caused an advection fog.[41]

According to the National Oceanic and Atmospheric Administration (NOAA), an advection fog is defined as a "fog that forms as warmer, moist air moves over a cold ground. The air is cooled to saturation by the loss of heat to the cold ground."[42]

With the mild weather and rise in temperature in early May, the warm air was cooled into dew and produced an advection fog upon meeting the snow-covered, cold earth. This phenomenon probably can explain the "exhalations" of vapors and atmospheric dust from the massive body of snow on the earth, as suggested by Viator[43] and a writer by the name of "Well-wisher."[44]

Mounting evidence showed that there were forest fires that caused smoke, soot, and ashes to collect in the air and frozen earth that cooled air near the surface. This resulted in advection fog as well as stagnancy of moisture and pollutants in the atmosphere. It is believed that the combination of these matters in the air conglomerated and caused the sudden darkness over New England.

THE MOON BECAME AS BLOOD

The appearance of a bloodred moon on the night of the Dark Day is now examined. According to one account, on the Dark Day, the moon was observed to be a nearly full moon. This is in accordance with the observation of a lunar eclipse on May 18, a day before the Dark Day.

On May 18, 1780, there was a partial lunar eclipse in the night sky. It was not a total lunar eclipse, but it was nearly total in the sense that most of the moon was eclipsed by the shadow of Earth. In fact, the lunar eclipse of May 18, 1780 is recorded as the "largest partial lunar eclipse" of the eighteenth century.[45] A night after the largest partial lunar eclipse, the moon still would have been nearly full, certainly not a half or crescent moon.

But what would have caused the nearly-full moon to appear bloodred? With so much atmospheric dust and pollutants in the atmosphere, the sunlight and the moonlight were blocked. But when the moon was finally visible, it appeared red like blood. This can be explained by the scattering of light as it passes through the particulate filled atmosphere.

In fact, this phenomenon is what causes the moon to appear reddish during total lunar eclipses as well. When the moon is completely overshadowed by Earth, the sun's rays that reach the moon do so by going through the Earth's atmosphere. However, the sun rays are scattered by the Earth's atmosphere on their way to the moon. Much particulate matter in the atmosphere, such as dust or clouds, scatter the shorter wavelength light rays and allow mostly the red-colored light rays to pass through. Thus, a reddish moon is observed during a total lunar eclipse. The same thing happens during sunset; as sun rays pass through the atmosphere, it is perceived as reddened sky.[46]

When there are more dust and pollutants in the atmosphere, even more of the light rays with shorter wavelength are scattered. As a result, the moon is perceived as deeper red in color. This is what most likely happened on the Dark Day—a concentrated collection of smoke, soot, and ashes combined with the fogs and clouds caused much light to be scattered, giving the moon a deeply reddened color. And when the New Englanders observed the moon, it appeared to have become like blood.

New England's Dark Day is interpreted to be the historical incident that corresponds to the sun becoming black and the moon as blood in the second half of Revelation 6:12. It is worth noting that among all the seals prophesied in the book of Revelation, the very first incident that took place in America is New England's Dark Day. As will be discussed later, more incidents will be related with America as she gets involved with some of the important prophecies in Revelation. Certainly, God is in control over the entire world—including America.

CHAPTER 11

THE SIXTH SEAL:
STARS OF HEAVEN FELL

THE LEONIDS

So far, two events of the sixth seal in Revelation have been interpreted: the great earthquake as the Great Lisbon Earthquake in 1755; and the sun becoming black and the moon as blood as New England's Dark Day in 1780. The next event in the sixth seal is described in verses 13 and 14a of chapter 6:

> [Rev 6:13] And the stars of heaven fell unto the earth, even as a fig tree casteth her untimely figs, when she is shaken of a mighty wind.

> [Rev 6:14a] And the heaven departed as a scroll when it is rolled together;

This description seems to illustrate an event such as meteor shower on a grand scale. Throughout history, mankind has seen many meteor showers and meteor storms. Yet, the prolific kinds are remembered with greater significance in history.

The superlative meteoric incident in history is the Leonids observed on November 13, 1833 under a clear sky over a vast area in North America. It consisted of such a profuse number of meteors falling from the heaven that it sparked new interests in the origins of meteors for people in the nineteenth century.

The meteor shower consisted of meteors of various sizes; some as large and bright as Jupiter, Venus, or the moon; some the size of an eighteen-pound cannon ball; and many like large balls of fire. The intensity of light that these meteors brought to the dark night sky was wondrous. Some were awakened from sleep due to the brightness of the sky. One observer noted that he "could distinguish the color of a man's beard" under the light of the meteors. Some could even "read common sized print, without much difficulty" under the light that was often whiter than the moonlight. The largest meteor, seen in Frederick, Maryland, was reported to have shone such an intense light that casted faint shadows in the night.[1]

As a result of the splendid shooting-star show, the meteoric phenomenon became a hot topic discussed with great attention in just about every conversation held within North America. Immediately after the Leonids occurred on November 13, people began to share their observations of the Leonids through newspapers to study and provide scientific explanations and theories about the phenomenon of meteor shower.[2] Thus was the beginning of organized study of meteor astronomy.[3]

The meteor shower such as the one observed on November 13, 1833 is called the Leonids because the origin of the meteors seemed to be the constellation Leo. Later in 1866, the comet associated with the Leonids was found to be the Comet Tempel-Tuttle. This comet was named after Ernst Tempel and Horace Tuttle, who not only discovered it but also calculated its orbit to be about thirty-three years. Simply put, the comet would return every thirty-three years, bringing with it prolific meteor shower.[4]

However, this comet was not rediscovered until the year 1965, and the Leonid storm associated with this comet were not observed until November 17, 1966. According to NASA, this meteor shower associated with the comet Tempel-Tuttle in 1966 "probably rivaled the historic showers observed in 1799 and 1833." Yes, there was another historic one observed in 1799, but there are not enough records to estimate the number of meteors fallen in 1799, and for some reason people were not inspired to investigate the origins of the meteors as opposed to the one in 1833.[5] The meteor storm of 1833 had truly superlative ramification.

There is much literature recounting observations of the Leonid shower of November 1833. Most notably, Denison Olmsted, a professor of mathematics and natural philosophy in Yale College, collected and organized various observations of the meteors. He published in 1834 an article, *Observations on the Meteors of November 13, 1833* in the *American Journal of Science and Arts*. He wrote in the beginning of the article:

The morning of November 13th, 1833, was rendered memorable by an exhibition of the phenomenon called SHOOTING STARS, which was probably more extensive and magnificent than any similar one hitherto recorded. The morning itself was, in most places where the spectacle was witnessed, remarkably beautiful. The firmament was unclouded; the air was still and mild; the stars seemed to shine with more than their wonted brilliancy . . . Probably no celestial phenomenon has ever occurred in this country, since its first settlement, which was viewed with so much admiration and delight by one class of spectators, or with so much astonishment and fear by another class.[6]

Like the Great Lisbon Earthquake in 1755 and New England's Dark Day in 1780, the reactions of the public when the prolific meteor shower occurred in 1833 included fear and astonishment. An observer from Bowling Green, Missouri, actually recounted that the citizens were forced to remind themselves of the following passage in the book of Revelation upon observing the meteors:[7]

[Rev 12:3] And there appeared another wonder in heaven; and behold a great red dragon, having seven heads and ten horns, and seven crowns upon his heads.

[Rev 12:4] And his tail drew the third part of the stars of heaven, and did cast them to the earth: and the dragon stood before the woman which was ready to be delivered, for to devour her child as soon as it was born.

According to the observer, if the passage were "a figurative expression, that figure appeared to be fully painted on the broad canopy of the sky,—spread over with sheets of light, and thick with streams of rolling fire. There was scarcely a space in the firmament which was not filled at every instant with these falling stars."[8]

The meteor shower was so magnificent and extravagant that people were instinctively reminded of the book of Revelation and end-time prophecies therein. Of course, this meteoric incident is the fulfillment of the prophecy in Revelation chapter 6 verse 13, not chapter 12.

The Leonids incident in 1833 also made the people to recall the verses of the sixth seal from Revelation chapter 6. An observer from Missouri wrote to describe the falling meteors: "Still at times they would shower down in groups—calling to mind the 'fig tree, casting her untimely figs when shaken by a mighty wind.'"[9]

According to the observations accounted by Professor Olmsted, the Leonids were seen in various parts of North America, reaching as far west as Missouri, as far east as the Atlantic coastline, north as far as Maine, and south as far as Louisiana, Alabama, and Georgia.[10]

Professor Olmsted also accounted the observations from vessels of New York harbor coming from various places, such as Europe, Liverpool, Rio Janeiro, Amsterdam, and Mobile through Gulf of Mexico. As extensive as his collection of the observations was from various parts of the world, Olmsted's article incorporated all the information gathered to describe the phenomenon of the Leonids in detail and with objectivity. According to London and other European correspondents, there were no meteor showers observed in their locations at the specified time.[11]

According to Olmsted's collective description of the Leonids in 1833, many who observed the falling meteors actually caught sight of it near or around 5 o'clock in the morning, when they woke up from sleep, either because they planned to wake up early or because they thought their dwellings were on fire due to the intense light of the meteors. Some of the observations were made by those who were out all night, and their observations are especially valuable as they provide the time when the meteor shower was first seen in the night sky.[12]

In Lynchburg, Virginia, the atmosphere had been uncommonly transparent since 10 o'clock of the previous night, the 12th, and shooting stars were first seen between 2 and 3 o'clock in the morning on the 13th. Meteors were first seen as early as 10 o'clock at night on the 12th in Salisbury, North Carolina, and at about 9 o'clock in Augusta, Georgia. In general, the meteors were first noticed between nine and twelve o'clock during the night time on the 12th, and their number and degree of intensity increased over time and reached their maximum about four o'clock in the morning on the 13th, and continued until they were no longer visible due to sunrise.[13]

The number of meteors seen on November 13, 1833 was astronomical and was nearly incomparable to any other meteor showers. In one part of Boston, an innumerable number of meteors were found falling from the sky. The observer described that when there were relatively less meteors in the sky, meteors "were falling about half as thick as the flakes of snow in one of our common snow falls, with intervals of a few seconds."[14]

He attempted to count the meteors about fifteen minutes before six o'clock in the morning, when there were much fewer meteors falling. He counted 650 stars in fifteen minutes in a small area in the sky, perhaps "a tenth part or rather less of the horizon," which meant that there were probably more than 8,660 meteors falling during the fifteen minutes in the entire sky he observed.[15]

According to Professor Olmsted, with further calculation, the meteors:

> . . . must have fallen at the rate of 34,640 an hour, making for three hours, 103,920. The observer mentions that the number had become fewer at the time of counting,

in consequence, probably of the advancing light of day. Reckoning, therefore, from 12, till 7 o'clock, we may safely double the foregoing amount, making the aggregate number of meteors 207,840,—an estimate which probably does not exceed, though it may fall very short of the whole number which were visible at Boston. On the supposition that the meteors seen at places remote from each other, were not the same, the entire number that descended towards the earth, must have been indefinitely great.[16]

THE HEAVEN DEPARTED AS A SCROLL

Not only did the number of meteors make the Leonids of 1833 famous and spectacular, but the unique pattern of the meteors falling from the sky unto the earth as well. The pattern was most unique in the sense that the shooting stars seemed to originate from a circular space in the heaven, located in the zenith according to some accounts or a little bit southeast from the zenith according to others. From one common center, meteors were observed to shoot off in all directions towards the horizon.[17]

In one of the accounts collected by Professor Olmsted, Mr. Alexander C. Twining, a civil engineer in West Point, New York, described this interesting phenomenon observed as follows:

There was a point a few degrees south and east of the zenith, which was evidently the directrix of all the apparent motions; and every luminous body, without exception, of those associated in the phenomenon, obeyed a regimen in relation to that point, which was such that every line and track of motion if continued backward, would have passed, as nearly as the eye could discern, through that specific point. In the vicinity of that point, a few star-like bodies were observed possessing very little motion and leaving very little length of trace; but, in their aspect, such as if a small nebula had softly swelled out from the heavens, gently elongated in its figure, and then as gently subsided. Farther off the motions were more rapid and the traces longer; and most rapid of all and longest in their trace, were those which originated but a few degrees above the horizon and descended down to it. In these, the aspect might be compared to that of flaming sparks driven swiftly athwart the sky by a strong wind . . . This point, of which mention has been made, cannot be supposed to have been a real part of space from which the luminous bodies actually proceeded, but the vanishing point of sight for motions which were truly or nearly parallel. If a multitude of bodies moving in parallel directions had entered the earth's atmosphere from that quarter of the heavens which has been pointed out, and become luminous by contact with the atmosphere, and had been dissipated by motions through it, they must have presented the apparent motions, very nearly, if not exactly, as those which I observed. The supposition is not suggested as a possible explanation of the facts, but as a guide to the conceptions of such as did not witness the phenomena, and may desire to have a clear idea of what they were. For, in the case supposed, if any luminous body were moving directly in the axis of vision, it would have appeared and vanished like a star without any apparent motion. Those which were near the axis of vision, would present the short trace and gentle motion of the nebulae described above; but according as that distance became greater, the apparent motion would be more rapid and the trace longer; and all the traces would be seen in directions diverging from the point in which the axis of vision met the heavens.[18]

Mr. Twining's description of this unique pattern of the dispersal of shooting stars from a common circular space in the heavens can be easily understood with the help of the image, Fig. 11-1.

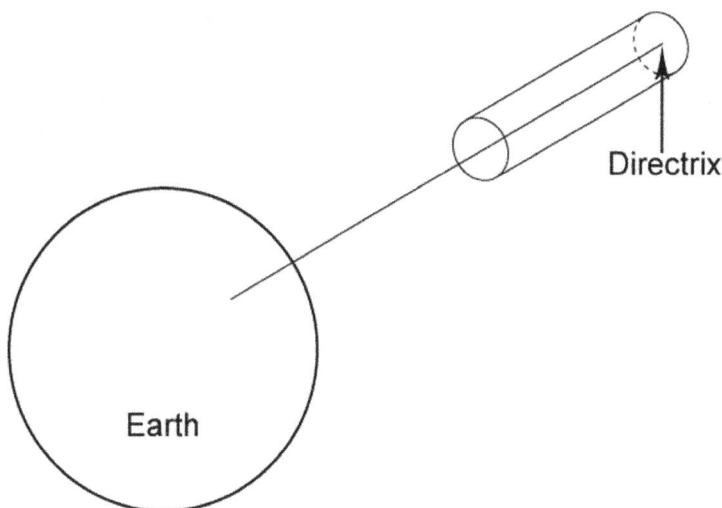

Fig. 11-1. Mr. Twining's illustrative description of the Leonids in 1833.

As illustrated in Figure 11-1, the base of the cylinder in the space above Earth is the "common circular space in heavens" where the meteors seemed to fall from, with the center point being the "directrix." Inside the circular area of the space, there were no meteors observed.

The height of the cylinder is a figurative measure, and represents the "axis of vision," where the stars travelled in paths parallel to each other.

People observed the meteors showering from heaven toward Earth starting at the circumference of the circular space and descending towards the horizon of Earth. Fig. 11-2 illustrates how the meteors were observed to start falling from the circumference of the circular space at the zenith.

Fig. 11-2. Simplified sketch of the meteors falling from a common circular space in heaven.

If seen from directly below the center of the circular space, the meteor shower would have provided a view as in Figure 11-2, with the white radiating lines representing the directions of the meteors falling, from the zenith towards the Earth's horizon. The periphery of the cylindrical space represents the "axis of vision" as Mr. Twining described in the excerpt above.

According to Mr. Twining's descriptions of the Leonids, the meteors stretched out in greater lengths as they neared the horizon of Earth. The meteors were of shorter length near the circular space, as if they were turning the direction of their descent from the "axis of vision" so that they were then visible after the turn. Of course, not all of the meteors were all visible in the immediate vicinity of the circular space; they became first visible at any point between the circular space and the Earth's horizon.

Many works of art depicting the Leonids in 1833 have been created since the meteor shower, which show this exact pattern of shooting stars observed by Mr. Twining. Fig. 11-3 is a woodcut printed image of the incident, illustrated by a man named Pickering who witnessed the meteor shower at Niagara Falls, New York.

As seen from the image, the shooting stars seemed to have originated from the circular space and fall towards the horizon of Earth. In fact, many testify that these meteors "descended quite to the earth," and came down "apparently almost to the house tops." Many meteors "seemed almost to strike the masts of the vessels" and, "while descending, it seemed as if some would fall upon the deck of the boat though none did." Most of them did not actually strike the ground, but seemed to be extinguished some distance from Earth.[19]

Fig. 11-3. Record of the Leonids in 1833 in the form of woodcut print illustration by Pickering.[20]

Interestingly, as much as this spectacular show of shooting stars aroused the senses of observers, who paid great attention to the whole phenomenon, no sound was heard that was associated with the meteors.[21]

So far, the descriptions of the meteors that fell on November 13, 1833 seem to agree with the descriptions of the sixth seal event in Revelation 6:13, "And the stars of heaven fell unto the earth, even as a fig tree casteth her untimely figs, when she is shaken of a mighty wind."

The directions of the majority of the meteors were from the directrix space towards the horizon of Earth, with many appearing to directly fall onto the houses and boats at ground level. It is interesting to note that the unique pattern of the meteor shower in 1833 also agrees with the description in the very following verse in Revelation about the sixth seal:

[Rev 6:14a] And the heaven departed as a scroll when it is rolled together;

Wasn't the phenomenon observed in the morning of November 13, 1833 and described exquisitely by Mr. Twining's "directrix" inside the circular space from which the meteors fell? Doesn't the anatomy of the cylindrical space that encases the "axis of vision" seem to match that of "a scroll when it is rolled together?" There is another verse from the Old Testament that describes almost the same as in Revelation 6:14. It is in Isaiah chapter 34 as follows:

[Isa 34:4] And all the host of heaven shall be dissolved, and the heavens shall be rolled together as a scroll: and all their host shall fall down, as the leaf falleth off from the vine, and as a falling fig from the fig tree.

Isn't this verse the similar depiction of the sixth seal event in Revelation 6:13–14a? The host of heaven represents the stars in heaven. The heaven, rolled together like a scroll, into a cylindrical anatomy, dissolved its host, where the word "to dissolve" (מָקַק, *maqaq*, *Strong* H4743) means to melt; to flow; to vanish; or to consume away.[22] The stars, as if they were leaves from the vine and figs from the fig tree, fell off from its main body. The falling of these innumerous heavenly hosts in scrolled up arrangement is Isaiah's description of meteor showers en route.

Such innumerable counts of meteors falling in uniform radiation from a common center were observed in a vast area of land, the northern limit being Concord, New Hampshire and Buffalo, New York, and the southern limit being the City of Washington, where the meteors fell exactly along the comet's trajectory, aligned with the "axis of vision." From the geographic location outside the limit—the limit set by the region directly under the circular base defined by the comet's circumference of the scrolled up cylinder along the directrix—the falling meteors would be observed as if scattering without pattern.[23] This affirms that Mr. Twining's analysis of the phenomenon is correct.

While according to many accounts, the meteors seemed to extinguish at some height before they reached the earth at ground level, other reports from various places about meteors having hit the ground are also interesting. People described the fallen substance of the meteors as lumps of animal jelly, "a mass of gelatinous matter" resembling soft soap in appearance.[24]

As mentioned earlier, another Leonid storm that was observed in the year 1799 had not caught much attention in papers as the one in 1833 did. There are some accounts about the Leonids in 1799, and it most likely does not fulfill the event of the sixth seal. The reason is because of the pattern of the shooting stars observed in the Leonids on November 12th,

1799. Unlike the pattern observed in the Leonids of 1833, the Leonids of 1799 consisted of meteors falling in the direction from North to South. They did not have a circular space in the heaven from which the meteors started falling towards the Earth's horizon that would match the description of a rolled up scroll.[25] Thus, only the Leonids of 1833 fit the description of the sixth seal.

CHAPTER 12

THE SIXTH SEAL: EVERY MOUNTAIN AND ISLAND MOVED

THE SUMATRA EARTHQUAKE

The next event in the sixth seal to discuss is in the latter part of Revelation 6:14. If the interpretation of the previous event as the Leonids on November 13, 1833 is correct, then the following event would have occurred after November 13, 1833.

As will be discussed in the next chapter, the seventh seal was opened in the year 1908. This means that the sixth seal would have occurred before 1908. What would be this incident? The Scripture describes it as follows:

[Rev 6:14b] and every mountain and island were moved out of their places.

What can make mountains and islands be moved out of their places? The first thing that comes to mind is a grand-scale earthquake with extraordinary magnitude.

On November 24, 1833, there was a great megathrust earthquake at Sumatra with an estimated magnitude between 8.8 and 9.2.[1] To understand why this particular earthquake could be interpreted as the event described in Revelation 6:14, some basic knowledge in seismology—the study of earthquakes—is necessary.

A megathrust earthquake is a grand-scale earthquake that occurs at a subduction zone. "Subduction is the process of the oceanic lithosphere colliding with and descending beneath the continental lithosphere."[2] At a subduction zone, two or more tectonic plates converge and form a boundary called a megathrust fault. The plate that is sitting underneath another plate is "subducted." When the tectonic plates suddenly slip from each other at this zone, a megathrust earthquake occurs.[3]

Why is this important to know? It is because all of the largest earthquakes in world's history are megathrust earthquakes[4] with moment magnitude scale around 9.0, occurring at subduction zones. In fact, it is known that only the megathrust earthquakes can cause such massive earthquakes.[5, 6] For example, during the recent historical earthquake in Japan on March 11, 2011, there was a slip of the Pacific tectonic plate subducting underneath the North American tectonic plate that created an earthquake of magnitude 9.0.[7] During the earthquake in Chile on February 27, 2010, there was a slip of the Nazca tectonic plate subducting underneath the South American tectonic plate and created an earthquake of magnitude 8.8.[8]

In the area west of Indonesia in the Indian Ocean and southeast of the country of India, there lies a subduction zone where the Indian and Australian tectonic plates subduct underneath the Eurasian tectonic plate. The subduction zone is known as the Sunda megathrust, which has its northern limits at Myanmar (Burma) and southern limits in Australia and runs along the southwestern coastlines of an Indonesian island called Sumatra.

This Sunda megathrust is one of the most seismogenic structures known on earth and causes vertical displacement or slipping of tectonic plates in the region during earthquakes. Historically, giant megathrust earthquakes have occurred in this region in the years 1797, 1833, 1861, 2004, 2005, and 2007, with the one that occurred in 1833 being the largest historical earthquake in this region before twenty-first century.[9]

There is another fault along the entire island of Sumatra called the "Great Sumatran Fault," which almost always contributes to the horizontal slipping of the tectonic plates during megathrust earthquakes in the western Indonesian region.[10] Together, the Sunda megathrust and Sumatran Fault form a highly oblique convergence of the tectonic plates at the latitudes of Sumatra.[11] As a result, the western coastline along the island of Sumatra is a highly seismogenic area and have caused great earthquakes throughout history, including the one in 1833.

When the megathrust earthquake hit the island of Sumatra on November 24, 1833, the earth shook terribly in the province of Bengkulu for five minutes and in the city of Padang for three minutes, both in the West Sumatra of Indonesia.[12] (The great earthquake on March 11, 2011 shook Japan for about three to five minutes.)[13]

The mega earthquake was felt throughout various places, and the shaking reached Singapore and Java. It was felt most severely along the coast of western Sumatra from Bengkulu to Pariaman, as well as near the Pagai islands. In the city of Pariaman, no one could remain standing during the earthquake. Among the affected areas, the greatest damage was done in the province of Bengkulu, where the shaking destroyed all structures.[14]

A great tsunami followed the earthquake and damaged "Bengkulu, Pulau Cinco, Indrapurah, Padang, and Pariaman" in Indonesia. The tsunami wave hit the coast in Padang at a height of three to four meters and swallowed houses, people, villages, and ships that were anchored at the beaches of West Sumatra. Because the settlement at the coastlines of West Sumatra was sparse and many people escaped the tsunami by climbing trees, there were fortunately not many casualties due to the tsunami. It has been reported that there was no death in Bengkulu and only one death in Padang.[15]

There are few historical accounts available about this mega earthquake in 1833.[16] However, with the ubiquity of coral reefs in the coasts of Sumatra, scientists today can easily determine the geological changes brought about by the mega earthquake in 1833.

Because the coral microatolls can survive under the water only, their coral skeletal growth pattern changes accordingly when the sea water level changes. If the sea water level rises, the microatolls grow outward and upward under water. If the sea water level lowers, the existing microatolls cannot grow upward anymore but can grow laterally only, as their growth is "limited by lowest water levels", and those exposed to sunlight for a prolonged time cannot grow but become dead fossils. Such fluctuations in their growth pattern and morphology according to the changes in lowest water levels allow precise dating of the geological changes that have occurred in the region. The microatoll skeleton records the changes in sea water levels as precisely "as a centimeter or two," and the dating of corals can be done up to "several hundred thousand years old" with the help of a technology called the "thermal ionization mass spectrometric (TIMS) U-series dating method."[17]

When late Holocene dates of coral death were examined from the year 1000 to 2000, the research showed that: "A histogram of the dates of coral death has a pronounced peak at 1832 . . . many of the emerged microatolls died suddenly between about 1820 and 1845. The coincidence of this cluster of coral deaths with 1833, the year of the giant earthquake, suggests strongly that these corals died from exposure due to emergence during that event."[18]

With the ability to obtain paleoseismic record of the earthquakes with available coral microatolls in the coasts of Sumatra, scientists have estimated that after the earthquake in 1833, there was an emergence of the Mentawai Islands in the subduction zone for about one or two meters as a result of thirteen-meter tectonic plates slipping at the subduction interface.[19]

What do these mean? The Mentawai Islands are the Sumatran outer-arc archipelago of seventy islands, including Sipora, North Pagai and South Pagai, and islets located west of mainland Sumatra. The Sunda trench is at the boundary formed by the tectonic plates of Sunda and Australia on the ocean floor where the subduction of plates occurs. By emergence, it means that there was a vertical uplift of the Mentawai Islands which increased towards the trench as a result of the giant earthquake at the Sunda megathrust, and "the 180 km of outer-arc ridge represented by the Pagai Islands and Sipora Islands experienced substantial uplift during the 1833 earthquake."[20]

In Fig. 12-1, the dark star illustrates the area of the December 26, 2004 earthquake, while the light star illustrates the area of the March 28, 2005 earthquake. As depicted in the figure, the Mentawai Islands located west of the Sumatra Island of Indonesia are the area affected by the November 25, 1833 mega earthquake. In addition to this vertical displacement of the affected area, a horizontal tilting was also observed, as the islands were tilted towards the mainland of West Sumatra after the mega earthquake in 1833.[21]

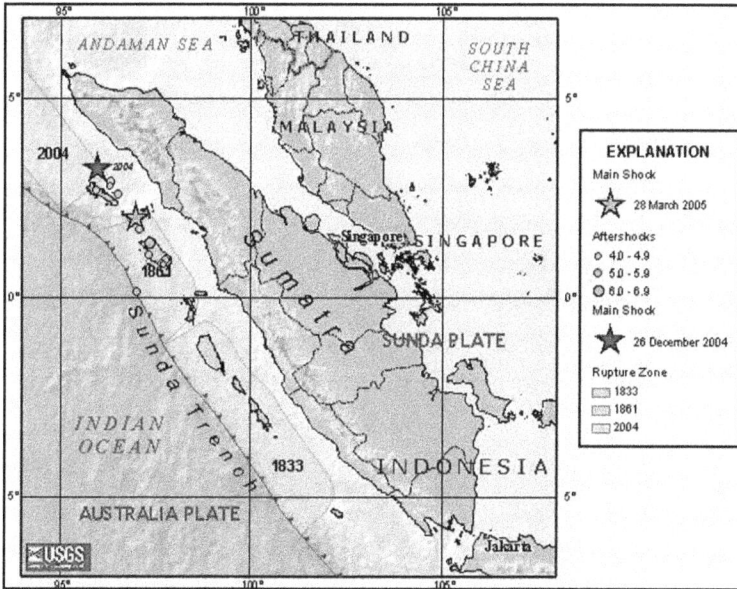

Fig. 12-1. Map of the Sunda Trench.[22]

If the earliest Sunda megathrust earthquakes were to be compared, the incident in 1833 outmatches that of 1797 in scale and magnitude. While the uplift, or emergence, of Sumatran outer arc islands experienced in 1797 only ranged from 0 to 80 cm, the measurements in 1833 were 1 to 3 m. The slip, or the rupture beneath the Mentawai islands, in 1797 ranged from 4 to 8 m, whereas the slip from 1833 were 7 to 18 m. The rupture extension of 1833 (170 to 550 km) also exceeded that of 1797 (160 to 370 km) as well as the estimated earthquake magnitude of 8.8 to 9.2 and 8.5 to 8.7 M_w, respectively.[23]

Therefore, the studies on coral microatolls conclude that the uplift amounts in 1797—the permanent displacements of geodetic vertical deformation—were "a factor of 2–3 smaller [compared to 1833] where the ruptures overlap" and "1797 slip averaged about 6 m [which is] about one half to one third the magnitude of slip along the 1833 rupture."[24] Conclusively, the earthquake of 1833 is appreciably greater than that of 1797, rendering much significance in history.

With such information, one can know that the islands were moved out of their places within the affected area of the great Sumatran earthquake, but only partly fulfilling the prophecy in Revelation 6:14b because these islands do not represent "every mountain and island" on Earth.

Therefore, another approach must be taken to interpret said mega earthquake as one of the possible candidate incidents that definitively fulfills the prophecy in Revelation 6:14b. The clue is in the magnitude of this mega earthquake which was so great that it most likely caused a shift in the Earth's axis. This is more than probable, since other megathrust earthquakes of similar magnitude have resulted in the shifting of the Earth's axis. Note that this is not the north-south axis of Earth, but "the axis about which Earth's mass is balanced."[25]

According to NASA, after the mega earthquake of magnitude 8.8 in Chile on Feb 27, 2010, the Earth's axis was shifted by 2.7 milliarcseconds (about 8 centimeters or 3 inches). As a result of the Chilean earthquake, the Earth's mass moved vertically and effectively shifted the Earth's figure axis. In addition, the length of day was estimated to be shortened by about 1.26 microseconds.[26]

Similarly, the magnitude 9.0 megathrust earthquake in Japan that occurred on March 11, 2011 resulted in shifting of the Earth's crust and axis.[27] During the megathrust earthquake in Japan, "the Pacific Plate shifted, actually moving under Japan at the Japan Trench", which caused the earthquake and tsunami that followed.[28]

According to NASA, the redistribution of the Earth's land masses due to the earthquake in Japan caused the Earth's axis to shift by about 6.5 inches and shortened the length of day by about 1.8 microseconds. Dr. Richard Gross, a research scientist in the Geodynamics and Space Geodesy Group at NASA's Jet Propulsion Laboratory, explained that the Earth's rotation changed due to the shifting of its axis, which was mainly due to the global displacement and rearrangement of mass. He further explained that with such great earthquakes, the movement of Earth can be measured as much as many feet at the epicenter of the earthquake, but "even a few thousand kilometers away, you can still have displacements of a millimeter or so."[29]

In principle, the displacement of the Earth's crust occurs on the other side of Earth as well, although such small amount of movement could not be visually measured. In Japan, one of the GPS stations actually moved thirteen feet from its position as a result of the mega earthquake.[30] In other words, an earthquake of such magnitude produces changes in locations of every land mass on Earth.

Advanced modern seismologic technology reveals that the massive earthquakes at the level of 9.0 magnitude occur at subduction zones, and when they do occur, they displace land masses throughout Earth and actually shift the Earth's axis as well as change the length of day. Such phenomenon, although not recorded, would most likely have also occurred when the megathrust earthquake hit the region west of Sumatra in Indonesia in November of 1833.

Therefore, dislocation of "every mountain and island" in Revelation 6:14b was manifested by the great megathrust earthquake that occurred on November 24, 1833 at the Sumatra.

FOR THE GREAT DAY OF HIS WRATH IS COME; AND WHO SHALL BE ABLE TO STAND?

In Revelation 6:15–17, the reactions of people to the events of the sixth seal are recorded.

[Rev 6:15] And the kings of the earth, and the great men, and the rich men, and the chief captains, and the mighty men, and every bondman, and every free man, hid themselves in the dens and in the rocks of the mountains;

[Rev 6:16] And said to the mountains and rocks, Fall on us, and hide us from the face of him that sitteth on the throne, and from the wrath of the Lamb:

[Rev 6:17] For the great day of his wrath is come; and who shall be able to stand?

In this passage, people who encountered the events of the sixth seal were frightened and tried to hide themselves in the dens and rocks of mountains from the wrath of God, believing that the great day of God's wrath has come.

After the Great Lisbon Earthquake in 1755, the Dark Day in New England in 1780, and the Leonid shower in 1833, people who witnessed the incidents generally had the attitude of being frightened and repenting before God, fearing God's wrath, and expecting His judgment at any moment. Whether or not such attitude was observed after the great Sumatran earthquake in 1833 remains unanswered.

After the Great Lisbon Earthquake in 1755, many political and religious leaders firmly held on to their belief that the earthquake was a punishment ordained by God, and insisted that people repent from their sins. There were, however, those with opposing views, and with their pursuit of scientific exploration of the cause of the earthquake, modern seismology was founded.

Similarly, there were many who believed in divine intervention of God when New England's Dark Day occurred in 1780. At the same time, there were many who sought scientific explanation of the preternatural darkness over New England by sharing their observations and discussing possible theories throughout New England communities.

After both the Great Lisbon Earthquake in 1755 and New England's Dark Day in 1780, many people introduced themselves to finding the natural causes and scientific explanations of the phenomena and started moving away from the spiritual explanations—ideas that such phenomena were divinely ordained.[31]

Ever since the birth of scientific inquiry for explaining the phenomena of natural disasters, earthquakes were gradually understood to be naturally occurring, not divinely ordained. Today, many insist that the natural disasters occurring on Earth are caused by lack of care for the mother Earth and abuse of the natural resources and landscapes.[32] These attitudes toward natural disasters are evidently different from those seen back in the eighteenth century.

When the earthquake in Lisbon and the Dark Day in New England occurred, the immediate response rendered by most of the survivors was repentance, fear, and respect for God as the Creator of the universe.

Today, about 250 years later, people generally believe that natural disasters are punishment from nature for humans' disrespect towards laws of nature. What a stark difference in attitude toward natural phenomena and God! Would people of all classes fear that the return of Jesus is near if a magnitude 9.0 scale earthquake, darkness phenomenon, or meteor shower occurred today, like they did in 1755 or 1780? Probably not.

Nowadays, it is much more natural for people to analyze catastrophic incidents scientifically and come up with preventive methods accordingly, with advanced technology and gigantic library of information available in all disciplines.

This obvious modern-day societal tendency increases the probability that the interpretation of the incidents of the eighteenth and early nineteenth centuries as the sixth seal is correct, as people back then readily feared God's wrath and His judgment day.

The Leonids observed on November 13, 1833 also infused fear in many people's minds and reminded them of the prophecy in the book of Revelation. This means that people became much alerted and anticipated the return of Jesus and the judgment day at any point in the near future. They had very similar, if not the same, mindset towards the manifested prophetic events as those who experienced New England's Dark Day in 1780.

In the eighteenth century, people were familiar with the Scriptures including the end-time prophecy, and when they witnessed complete darkness throughout the day and half, they gathered at meetinghouses for prayer and fearfully waited for the judgment day that they believed was imminent.

It is interesting to note that while people in 1755 debated as an important religious and political issue whether the great earthquake was directed by God to punish humans or naturally caused, people in 1780 and 1833 took the debate further and anticipated the judgment day to be near. As in Revelation 6:15–16, people who experienced the Great Lisbon Earthquake of 1755 were fearful of the wrath of the Lamb, believing that the earthquake was a punishment from God, and repented their sins. People who experienced New England's Dark Day of 1780 and the Leonid shower of 1833 feared that the judgment day, or as in Revelation 6:17, "the great day of his wrath [had] come," so they believed the end time prophecies were being fulfilled before them and tried to listen attentively for the sound of the last trumpet and the return of Jesus. As such, even the responses of people who witnessed the events of the sixth seal seem to have been made in the order as described in verses 15 through 17!

Assuming the natural response of people who experienced the megathrust earthquake in Sumatra in November 1833 was fear, it suffices to say that all four events of the sixth seal induced great fear in people's minds.

Why is it important to interpret the events of the sixth seal? What makes such interpretation of these events reasonable and probable? Regarding the sixth seal, the interpretations rendered that the first event was in 1755, second in 1780, third on November 13, 1833, and fourth on November 24, 1833. Amazingly, these four incidents actually occurred in the order that they are written in the Scripture within a timeframe.

Certainly, giant earthquakes have occurred at different times and locations throughout history, and Leonid meteor showers could occur every thirty-three years, based on the orbit of the comet Tempel-Tuttle. Nonetheless, what is amazing is that the probability of such four separate events of the sixth seal all occurring together in a sequence within a specific timeframe in history is most likely very low. In addition, the search yielded three of the four historical incidents showing records of people fearing God's wrath and judgment. Could this just be a mere coincidence?

On a final note, what is the significance of the sixth seal? Some may think that the last event in the sequence of the sixth seal happened in a remote and uninhabited area of Sumatra. However, if the sixth seal events are seen in full sequence, it could reveal God's fascinating directive. Starting from Lisbon in Europe, followed by two incidents in North America across the Atlantic Ocean, and finishing at the opposite side of the globe in outer Sumatra in Southeast Asia, the sixth seal events suggest that the Gospel, the Good News of God, will be propagated to the remotest areas of Earth, and that Christianity will be found in all corners of Earth. This will be further confirmed through the interpretation of the two events that occur between the sixth and the seventh seals in the next volume.

CHAPTER 13

THE SEVENTH SEAL: A GOLDEN CENSER WITH FIRE

THE TUNGUSKA BLAST

Next interpretation is on the seventh seal. It is the last seal in the series that was opened before sounding the seven trumpets, the next phase of prophecies in Revelation. What characterize the seventh seal, the seventh trumpet, and the seventh bowl are the common natural phenomena, such as voices, thunderings, lightnings, and an earthquake. A scrutinizing of the Scriptures is needed to identify the differences among the three distinct events in Revelation. Regarding the seventh seal, the Scripture states as follows:

> [Rev 8:5] And the angel took the censer, and filled it with fire of the altar, and cast it into the earth: and there were voices, and thunderings, and lightnings, and an earthquake.

Notice that in verse 5, voices, thunderings, lightnings, and an earthquake followed the opening of the seventh seal. With these in mind, the Scripture describing the seventh trumpet is examined, which states as follows:

[Rev 11:19] And the temple of God was opened in heaven, and there was seen in his temple the ark of his testament: and there were lightnings, and voices, and thunderings, and an earthquake, and great hail.

Notice that in verse 19, there are lightnings, voices, thunderings, and an earthquake, just as in the seventh seal. Notice also that there is another natural phenomenon that is added in the seventh trumpet—great hail. This is a natural phenomenon that is not included in the seventh seal, but included in the seventh trumpet; a pattern worth noticing. Now, the Scripture describing the seventh bowl is examined, which states as follows:

[Rev 16:18] And there were voices, and thunders, and lightnings; and there was a great earthquake, such as was not since men were upon the earth, so mighty an earthquake, and so great.

[Rev 16:19] And the great city was divided into three parts, and the cities of the nations fell: and great Babylon came in remembrance before God, to give unto her the cup of the wine of the fierceness of his wrath.

[Rev 16:20] And every island fled away, and the mountains were not found.

[Rev 16:21] And there fell upon men a great hail out of heaven, every stone about the weight of a talent: and men blasphemed God because of the plague of the hail; for the plague thereof was exceeding great.

Notice that in verse 18, there are voices, thunders, and lightnings, just as in the seventh seal and the seventh trumpet. In addition, there is a great earthquake in the seventh bowl, so great that such magnitude had never been seen in human history. There is also great hail that fell out of heaven that was so great that men blasphemed God because of the plague. These catastrophes—the greatest earthquake and possibly the greatest hail—are not part of the seventh seal and the seventh trumpet.

Other than voices, thunders, and lightnings, there is an earthquake but no hail in the seventh seal; there is an earthquake with great hail in the seventh trumpet; and there is a great earthquake and great hail in the seventh bowl. Such are the differences to keep in mind when dealing with the seventh seal, the seventh trumpet, and the seventh bowl. After scrutinizing the details of the seventh seal, the findings will be applied to interpreting the seventh trumpet in detail in volume 2.

For the discussion of the seventh seal, the Scripture must be thoroughly understood:

[Rev 8:1] And when he had opened the seventh seal, there was silence in heaven about the space of half an hour.

[Rev 8:2] And I saw the seven angels which stood before God; and to them were given seven trumpets.

[Rev 8:3] And another angel came and stood at the altar, having a golden censer; and there was given unto him much incense, that he should offer it with the prayers of all saints upon the golden altar which was before the throne.

[Rev 8:4] And the smoke of the incense, which came with the prayers of the saints, ascended up before God out of the angel's hand.

[Rev 8:5] And the angel took the censer, and filled it with fire of the altar, and cast it into the earth: and there were voices, and thunderings, and lightnings, and an earthquake.

[Rev 8:6] And the seven angels which had the seven trumpets prepared themselves to sound.

The opening of the seventh seal involves proceedings in the heaven as described in verses 2 through 4 and 6. The effects of the seventh seal on the earth are described in verse 5, which are occurrences of voices, thunderings, lightnings, and an earthquake after the angel took a golden censer in verse 3 and filled it with fire of the altar and cast it into the earth in verse 5. Before affirming the interpretation of this event in history, an event consisting of these natural phenomena must first be identified.

The interpretation starts with narrowing down of the time frame during which the seventh seal could have occurred. The event would have occurred between the sixth seal and the first trumpet. The last event of the sixth seal occurred in November 1833, and, as will be discussed in volume 2, the first trumpet was sounded in 1914. If these interpretations are correct, the seventh seal event is expected to have occurred between the years 1833 and 1914.

Between 1833 and 1914, there was an event in history that seemed to involve the phenomena described in Revelation 8:5— a golden censer filled with fire cast from heaven to earth, voices, thunderings, lightnings, and an earthquake. This event was the Tunguska event, a mysterious explosion that occurred in the atmosphere over the Central Siberian Plateau in the morning of June 30, 1908. A little past seven o'clock in the morning, local residents witnessed a fireball crossing the sky over them and exploding in the air shortly afterwards, producing heat, shock waves, loud "gunfire-like sounds," thunderings, bright nights, magnetic storm, and an earthquake. This incident sparked curious debate on its origin among scientists that still remains unanswered today.[1]

Since the explosion in 1908, scientists have come up with various explanations for the Tunguska event. The scientific notion most accepted today is that the mysterious fireball was either a comet, a meteorite, or an asteroid in origin.[2, 3] The identification of the exact matter that caused the Tunguska event still awaits scientific confirmation. Nevertheless, for the purposes of discussion of the event in this book, the mysterious object that exploded in central Siberia will be referred to as a meteorite.

The Tunguska blast is famous for being "the largest meteoroid impact known in the Earth's recent history" according to Dr. Alexander Bagrov, a leading research associate doctor of physics and mathematics at the Astronomy Institute of the Russian Academy of Sciences. Because the same magnitude of power as the Tunguska blast could have easily destroyed any densely populated cities throughout Europe, the Tunguska event has raised a meteorological concern related to human life on Earth.[4]

In fact, according to Dr. Bagrov, if the meteorite's trajectory had been longer, delaying the explosion by 4 hours and 47 minutes, then St. Petersburg, the capital of the Russian Empire at the time, would have been wiped out, causing a high death toll. While various scientists have made such predictions throughout history, the Tunguska meteorite has been cited as "the milestone in terrestrial history" which alerted scientists of the catastrophic hazards that would be imposed on Earth by meteorite or asteroid impacts.[5]

Scientific expeditions and investigations of the Tunguska blast allowed scientists to come up with possible theories on the cause of the blast. Much of the data collected about the Tunguska event were based on testimonies from survivors of the blast and eyewitnesses of strangely bright nights or earthquakes in different parts of the world. Records of many such eyewitness stories uniformly and collectively support the factual data obtained from the expeditions of the Tunguska site.[6]

According to many accounts and records, the Tunguska event began with an explosion at "7:14 a.m. local time." The "exact location of the epicenter" of the blast is known to be at "latitude 60 degrees 55 minutes north, longitude 101 degrees 57 minutes east." The meteorite was observed "over an area 1,500 kilometers across." The fireball was so bright that some eyewitnesses described it as bright as the sun. The explosion happened "in mid-air, between 5 and 10 kilometres above the ground," with the energy of "between 10 and 20 megatons." This magnitude of energy is about one thousand times more powerful than the atomic bomb that hit Hiroshima during the World War II.[7, 8]

Although there was a massive explosion in the air, there was no impact crater or fireball remnants found on the ground under the epicenter of the explosion. This means that there was no object or its fragments hitting the ground, exhausting entirely in mid-air. The explosion, however, was so massive that its shock wave flattened trees over an area of 2,150 square kilometers. At ground zero, around two hundred square kilometers of forest were burned by its heat.[9]

The heat and shock waves of the explosion were felt seventy kilometers away from the epicenter in the city of Vanavara. Seven hundred kilometers away, people wondered at the "bright lights in the sky." One thousand two hundred kilometers away, people became scared from hearing "loud explosions, like gunfire." In addition to generating "a local magnetic storm," the blast shook the atmosphere and the earth, causing an earthquake with magnitude 5.0 on the Richter scale. Seismic waves were detected and recorded at various parts of the world. In Europe and Asia, night skies remained bright for several days.[10]

Such are the data pertaining to the Tunguska blast that have been collected and verified by various scientists who lived throughout the twentieth century. These strange phenomena that occurred with the Tunguska blast seem to match the descriptions of the events of the seventh seal in Revelation 8:5.

The loud sounds of explosions that were similar to those of gunfire were probably the "voices" in verse 5. Those who witnessed the Tunguska event also heard thundering sounds in the sky, which confirms the fulfilled prophecy of "thunderings" in verse 5. The spectacle of bright lights observed far from the epicenter of the event was most likely the fulfillment of the prophecy of "lightnings" in verse 5. The seismic waves that shook the earth were most likely the fulfillment of the prophecy of "an earthquake" in verse 5.

Eyewitness details of the Tunguska event readily testify the fulfillment of the prophetic events of the seventh seal in the book of Revelation. The following account details the censer filled with fire of the altar being cast into the earth by the angel, as in verse 5:

> Suddenly a blindingly bright pillar of fire, the size of a tall office building, races across the clear blue sky. The dazzling fireball moves within a few seconds from the south-southeast to the north-northwest, leaving a thick trail of light some 800 kilometres long. It descends slowly for a few minutes and then explodes about 8 kilometres above the ground. The explosion lasts only a few seconds but it is so powerful . . .[11]

The Tunguska fireball radiated much heat to its surroundings. Indeed, the trees at ground zero were burned and the local residents felt as if their clothes and body parts were burning.[12] If Tunguska's mysterious fireball was the golden censer that was filled with fire of the altar and cast into the earth by the angel, then the heat of the fire must have caused these effects.

When the shock waves of the explosion reached the city of Vanavara, a resident sitting in his porch suddenly found himself flying out of his chair. As he felt the enormous heat wave, he almost mistook that his shirt was burning. Right before losing his consciousness, he witnessed the "bright blue 'tube' that covered an enormous part of the sky." Then he woke up to the sounds that shook and destroyed his house and barn, including windows. Another resident ran into his house as soon as he felt the heat waves burning his ears. There, he "[heard] thunder disappearing to the north" as he helplessly watched parts of his house falling apart.[13]

The shock waves traveled further north and threw the tents and their occupants off the ground. Many were injured, and an elder died from shock. Herds of reindeer were killed by the fire in forests. Two hundred kilometers to the south, a farmer "[heard] sudden bangs, as if from gunfire. His horse [fell] on its knees." Lest his plough would fly away with the shock wave, he held onto it tight. Around him, trees were bent, soil stormed away, and "a wall of water" shoot up the river.[14]

Six hundred kilometers southwest of the epicenter, the Trans-Siberian express train came to a sudden stop as the train and the tracks started shaking violently. Shocked with fear, passengers shuddered at "the loud bursts of noises" that followed with "sounds of distant thunder." Seven hundred kilometers to the west of the explosion, "bright lights in the sky" were seen, and one thousand two hundred kilometers away, "loud explosions, like gunfire" were heard "for several minutes."[15]

On the evening of the Tunguska blast, "bright, colourful and prolonged dusks were noticed across the Continent as far as Spain." The night sky in the British Isles was "unusually bright." Citizens of Antwerp observed "the northern horizon appeared to be on fire" after the sun had set. These strange bright nights continued for a few days and disappeared.[16]

According to *the Times*, people were able to "read a newspaper in the open air" in London, Dublin, and Berlin. In London, people actually called the police thinking that the city was on fire. The Royal Observatory at Greenwich reported in its magazine that the sky was filled with "brilliant red" color that "photographs of terrestrial objects" could be taken at night.[17]

Nocturnal glows were observed for several nights following the Tunguska blast in various colors—ruddy ones in Berlin,

Germany, light blue night sky with pink touching the clouds in London (that actually made people think that London was on fire), bright nights in Bristol of England, brilliant red horizon in Greenwich, England, and "a peculiar strong orange-yellow light over the horizon" with "more yellow in its higher parts . . . over northern Europe and the United States."[18] These colorful glows seen in the night skies in vast areas of the world following the Tunguska blast may be interpreted as the "lightnings" in Revelation 8:5.

At this point, the definition of the word "lightnings" should be clearly understood. Lightnings, as commonly understood, is what usually accompanies thunders. From this standpoint, the word "lightnings" does not necessarily describe the nocturnal glows in the sky. However, the original Greek word for "lightning" (ἀστραπή, *astrapē*) in verse 5 also means "bright shining"[19] as that of a candle in Luke 11:36. The Tunguska blast broke the darkness and shone the night skies with brightness. Therefore, the nightly glows that accompanied the Tunguska blast for several days in various parts of Europe and Asia do not come short of consummating the prophecy of "lightnings."

According to local eyewitnesses, loud sounds similar to gunfire were heard, and they were clearly distinguishable from thundering sounds. Distinct from each other, the "gunfire-like sounds" and the "thundering sound" that accompanied the Tunguska blast are most likely the "voices" and "thunders" that John wrote about in the book of Revelation, respectively. The original Greek word for "voices" (φωνή, *phōnē*) in verse 5 does not only mean "the sound of uttered words" but also "a sound, tone: of inanimate things, as of musical instruments."[20] It can be a tone that is "articulate, bestial or artificial."[21] The usage of this particular meaning can be seen in various Scriptures, some of which are shown below in italicized font:

[Mt 24:31] And he shall send his angels with a great *sound* of a trumpet, and they shall gather together his elect from the four winds, from one end of heaven to the other.

[Jn 3:8] The wind bloweth where it listeth, and thou hearest the *sound* thereof, but canst not tell whence it cometh, and whither it goeth: so is every one that is born of the Spirit.

[1Co 14:7] And even things without life giving *sound*, whether pipe or harp, except they give a distinction in the sounds, how shall it be known what is piped or harped?

[1Co 14:8] For if the trumpet give an uncertain *sound*, who shall prepare himself to the battle?

[Rev 1:15] And his feet like unto fine brass, as if they burned in a furnace; and his voice as the *sound* of many waters.

[Rev 9:9] And they had breastplates, as it were breastplates of iron; and the *sound* of their wings *was* as the *sound* of chariots of many horses running to battle.

[Rev 18:22] And the voice of harpers, and musicians, and of pipers, and trumpeters, shall be heard no more at all in thee; and no craftsman, of whatsoever craft *he be,* shall be found any more in thee; and the *sound* of a millstone shall be heard no more at all in thee;

As can be seen in the Scriptures above, the word "voices" (φωνή, *phōnē*) in the Bible does not always mean human voice. It can refer to the sounds of many different things, be it a millstone, waters, chariots, wings, harp, trumpet, or wind. Tunguska's strange gunfire-like sounds that scared people can also be described as "voices," and this is most likely the case.

Records indicate that the "earthquake" in Revelation 8:5 was also fulfilled with the Tunguska blast. Seismic waves were registered at several earthquake-measuring stations around the world, including in St. Petersburg.[22] The magnitude of the seismic activity was equivalent to Richter scale 5.0 of an earthquake.[23] The shock waves created by changes in atmospheric pressure were observed to have raced around Earth two times.[24]

Finally, the Tunguska fireball exploded in the air, leaving no impact crater. In the seventh seal, the angel cast it "into the earth" (εἰς τὴν γῆν, *eis tēn gēn*). The preposition εἰς (*eis;* into), in general, denotes "entrance into, or direction and limit: into, to, towards, for, among."[25] Although it can mean that the fire entered and penetrated the earth, here, it is more probable that it was just cast towards the earth. Moreover, the Scripture does not explicitly describe that the fireball ended up touching the earth. In the seventh trumpet, however, there is an explicit expression about the "great hail," signifying a direct impact with Earth's crust. The following Scripture pertains to the seventh trumpet:

[Rev 11:19] And the temple of God was opened in heaven, and there was seen in his temple the ark of his testament: and there were lightnings, and voices, and thunderings, and an earthquake, and *great hail.*

With all the accounts and evidence, it can be said that the seventh seal was executed exactly as it was prophesied in Revelation.

SOVEREIGN GOD IN CONTROL

A lot of effort was put into providing scientific evidence to explain various phenomena of the seals. Many of them would and could be explained using human reasoning and the scientific approach, but behind the saga is God's transcending divine workmanship at hand. Through the sequence of these events, the sovereign God wished mankind to repent from wickedness, to believe in Him, and to know that the return of His Son is approaching ever nearer.

Between Revelation chapters 6 and 8, where the sixth and seventh seals are written respectively, there are two more events in chapter 7: the sealing of 144,000 children of Israel and the appearing of a great multitude of people from all the nations. The seven trumpets, along with these two events, will be expounded on in volume 2.

Also, the topics of the rapture, the Antichrist, and the wars in the last 3.5 years will be dealt with in details in consecutive volumes.

ENDNOTES

PREFACE

1. "Bill Text Versions, 111th Congress (2009-2010), H.R.3200," *The Library of Congress, THOMAS*, accessed January 14, 2013, http://thomas.loc.gov/cgi-bin/query/z?c111:H.R.3200:.

CHAPTER 1

1. Joseph H. Thayer, *Thayers' Greek English Lexicon of the New Testament* (Peabody, MA: Hendrickson, 1889).
2. The "vials" in the King James Version are translated into "bowls" in other versions of the Bible. Throughout the text of this book, we use the term "bowls" to describe the seven plagues in Revelation chapter 16.
3. "Pregnancy Symptom: Contractions," *Pregnancy Information Center*, MedHelp, accessed October 5, 2011, http://www.medhelp.org/tags/health_page/28/Pregnancy/Pregnancy-Symptom-Contractions?hp_id=1055.

CHAPTER 2

1. Joseph H. Thayer, *Thayers' Greek English Lexicon of the New Testament* (Peabody, MA: Hendrickson, 1889).

2. *Ibid.*
3. *Ibid.*
4. Marvin R. Vincent, *Vincent's Word Studies in the New Testament* (Peabody, MA: Hendrickson, 1888).
5. Adam Clarke, *Adam Clarke's Commentary on the Bible* (New York: Abingdon, 1829).
6. Albert Barnes, *Albert Barnes' Notes on the Bible* (Grand Rapids: Baker, 1885).
7. "Pestilence," *Dictionary.com Unabridged,* accessed February 23, 2012, http://dictionary.reference.com/browse/pestilence.
8. "Bubonic Plague," *Dictionary.com Unabridged,* accessed February 23, 2012, http://dictionary.reference.com/browse/bubonic plague.
9. Thayer, *Greek English Lexicon of the New Testament.*
10. *Ibid.*
11. Robert Jamieson, A. R. Fausset, and David Brown, *A Commentary on the Old and New Testaments* (1871).
12. Vincent, *Vincent's Word Studies in the New Testament.*
13. John Aberth, *The Black Death: The Great Mortality of 1348-1350: A Brief History with Documents* (Boston, MA: Bedford/St. Martin's, 2005).
14. Stephanie Haensch, Raffaella Bianucci, Michel Signoli, Minoarisoa Rajerison, Michael Schultz, Sacha Kacki, Marco Vermunt, Darlene A. Weston, Derek Hurst, Mark Achtman, Elisabeth Carniel, and Barbara Bramanti, "Distinct Clones of Yersinia Pestis Caused the Black Death," *PLoS Pathog* 6.10 (2010), accessed February 22, 2012, http://journals.plos.org/plospathogens/article?id=10.1371/journal.ppat.1001134.

15. Nicholas Wade, "Europe's Plagues Came from China, Study Finds," *New York Times,* October 31, 2010, accessed February 22, 2012, http://www.nytimes.com/2010/11/01/health/01plague.html.

16. Suzanne Austin Alchon, *A Pest in the Land: New World Epidemics in a Global Perspective* (Albuquerque: U of New Mexico, 2003), 21.

17. "Plague," *Centers for Disease Control and Prevention*, November 18, 2014, accessed May 7, 2015, http://www.cdc.gov/plague/history/.

18. Justus Friedrich Carl Hecker, Trans., Benjamin Guy Babington, *The Epidemics of the Middle Ages*, 3d ed. (London: Trübner, 1859).

19. *Ibid.*

20. *Ibid.*

21. "Beast," *Dictionary.com Unabridged,* accessed February 23, 2012, http://dictionary.reference.com/browse/beast.

22. James Strong, *Strong's Hebrew and Greek Dictionaries* (1890).

23. Thayer, *Greek English Lexicon of the New Testament.*

24. *Ibid.*

25. Joseph Patrick Byrne, *The Black Death* (Westport, Conn.: Greenwood, 2004).

26. Wade, "Europe's Plagues Came From China, Study Finds."

27. Byrne, *Black Death.*

28. Karl S. Kruszelnicki, "Black Death," *ABC News,* September 13, 2007, accessed May 8, 2015, http://www.abc.net.au/science/articles/2007/09/13/2031252.htm?site=galileo/greatmomentsinscience&topic=latest.

29. Alchon, *A Pest in the Land: New World Epidemics in a Global Perspective.*

30. Credit: © Timemaps, CC BY-SA 3.0, accessed May 8, 2015, http://commons.wikimedia.org/wiki/File:Spread-Of-The-Black-Death.gif. Size changed.

31. George D. Sussman, "Was the Black Death in India and China?" *Bulletin of the History of Medicine* 85.3 (2011): 319-55, accessed May 8, 2015, http://www.ncbi.nlm.nih.gov/pubmed/22080795.

32. Lakshmikanthan Anandavalli, "The Black Death in Medieval India: A Historical Mystery, Tangents," *Tangents, The Journal of the Master of Liberal Arts Program at Stanford University* 6 (2007): 20-25, accessed May 8, 2015, http://mla.stanford.edu/sites/default/files/shared/documents/Tangents07.pdf.

33. Peter Jay, "A Distant Mirror: Europe's Black Death Is a History Lesson in Human Tragedy – and Economic Renewal," *TIME Europe,* July 17, 2000: 3.

34. "World Population: Historical Estimates of World Population," *U.S. Census Bureau,* accessed May 9, 2015, http://www.census.gov/population/international/data/worldpop/table_history.php.

35. "World, The World Factbook," *Central Intelligence Agency,* accessed May 9, 2015, https://www.cia.gov/library/publications/the-world-factbook/geos/xx.html.

36. "Antarctica, The World Factbook," *Central Intelligence Agency,* accessed May 9, 2015, https://www.cia.gov/library/publications/the-world-factbook/geos/ay.html.

CHAPTER 3

1. Joseph H. Thayer, *Thayers' Greek English Lexicon of the New Testament* (Peabody, MA: Hendrickson, 1889).
2. Henry S. Lucas, "The Great European Famine of 1315, 1316, and 1317," *Speculum* 5.4 (1930): 343-77.
3. *Ibid.*
4. *Ibid.*
5. *Ibid.*
6. *Ibid.*
7. *Ibid.*
8. *Ibid.*
9. *Ibid.*
10. *Ibid.*
11. *Ibid.*
12. *Ibid.*
13. *Ibid.*
14. *Ibid.*
15. *Ibid.*
16. Ralph A. Graves, "Fearful Famines of the Past, History Will Repeat Itself Unless the American People Conserve Their Resources," *National Geographic Magazine* 32.1 (1917).
17. *Ibid.*
18. Judith E. Walsh, *A Brief History of India* (Infobase, 2006), 292.
19. Shankarlal C. Bhatt and Gopal K. Bhargava, eds., *Land and People of Indian States and Union Territories: Uttar Pradesh*, Vol. 28 (Kalpaz Publications, 2006), 21.
20. Ian Wilson, "Can We Predict the Next Indian Mega-Famine?" *J. Energy and Environment* 20.1-2 (2009): 11-24.

21. "List of Famines," *Wikipedia*, accessed September 22, 2011, http://en.wikipedia.org/wiki/List_of_famines.
22. Lucas, "The Great European Famine of 1315, 1316, and 1317."

CHAPTER 4

1. Matthew White, "Selected Death Tolls for Wars, Massacres and Atrocities Before the 20th Century," *Necrometrics*, accessed February 2, 2012, http://necrometrics.com/pre1700a.htm#European.
2. Graziella Caselli, Jacques Vallin, and Guillaume J. Wunsch, *Demography: Analysis and Synthesis; A Treatise in Population Studies* (Academic, 2006), 34.
3. Bill Blakemore, "'The Great Big Book of Horrible Things': WWII and Climate Change," *ABC News*, May 20, 2012, accessed May 6, 2015, http://abcnews.go.com/blogs/technology/2012/05/the-great-big-book-of-horrible-things-wwii-and-climate-change.
4. Bill Marsh, "Population Control, Marauder Style," *The New York Times*, November 6, 2011, accessed May 6, 2015, http://www.nytimes.com/imagepages/2011/11/06/opinion/06atrocities_timeline.html?ref=sunday.
5. John Man, *Kublai Khan* (London: Bantam, 2007), 21.
6. Credit: © Astrokey 44, CC BY-SA 3.0, accessed May 6, 2015, http://commons.wikimedia.org/wiki/File:Mongol_Empire_map.gif, Size changed.
7. Man, *Kublai Khan*, 216.
8. "Genghis Khan the GREEN: Invader Killed so Many People That Carbon Levels Plummeted," *MailOnline*,

January 25, 2011, Associated Newspapers Ltd., accessed May 10, 2015, http://www.dailymail.co.uk/sciencetech/article-1350272/Genghis-Khan-killed-people-forests-grew-carbon-levels-dropped.html.

9. Vaclav Smil, *Why America Is Not a New Rome* (MIT, 2010), 62.

10. "History's Ten Largest Empires - Very Short History," *Very Short History RSS*, April 1, 2015, accessed May 9, 2015, http://veryshorthistory.com/154/historys-top-ten-empires.

11. Robert Finlay, *The Pilgrim Art: Cultures of Porcelain in World History* (Berkeley: U of California, 2010), 151.

12. "What Day Most Changed the Course of History?" *Atlantic*, March 1, 2011, accessed May 9, 2015, http://www.theatlantic.com/magazine/archive/2013/03/the-big-question/309238/.

13. Sam Harris, "The End of World Violence?" *The Daily Beast*, October 3, 2011, accessed May 9, 2015, http://www.thedailybeast.com/articles/2011/10/03/steven-pinker-talks-end-of-violence-with-sam-harris.html.

14. Ferris Jabr, "Steven Pinker: Humans Are Less Violent than Ever," *New Scientist*, October 21, 2011.

15. Robert I Rotberg, *Population History and the Family: A Journal of Interdisciplinary History Reader* (Cambridge, Mass.: MIT, 2001), 83.

16. Caselli et al., *Demography: Analysis and Synthesis; A Treatise in Population Studies.*

17. "World Population: Historical Estimates of World Population," *U.S. Census Bureau*, accessed May

9, 2015, http://www.census.gov/population/ international/data/worldpop/table_history.php.

18. Finlay, *The Pilgrim Art: Cultures of Porcelain in World History.*

19. Mike Ibeji, "Black Death: The Disease," *BBC,* February 17, 2011, accessed May 11, 2015, http:// www.bbc.co.uk/history/british/middle_ages/ blackdisease_01.shtml.

20. Alice Park, "The Black Death Bacterium Decoded," *Time,* October 13, 2011, accessed February 22, 2012, http://healthland.time.com/2011/10/13/the-black-death-bacterium-decoded.

21. "Turning Point Descriptions:" *NYSED Global History and Geography Online Resource Guide,* New York State Education Department, accessed May 11, 2015, http://www.p12.nysed.gov/ciai/socst/ ghgonline/turnpoint/textbox_descriptions.html.

22. Steve Connor, "How Climate Change Helped Genghis Khan: Scientists Believe a Sudden Period of Warmer Weather Allowed the Mongols to Invade with Such Success," *The Independent,* March 10, 2014, accessed May 12, 2015, http://www.independent. co.uk/news/science/how-climate-change-helped-genghis-khan-scientists-believe-a-sudden-period-of-warmer-weather-allowed-the-mongols-to-invade-with-such-success-9182580.html.

CHAPTER 5

1. A. T. Robertson, *Word Pictures in the New Testament* (Nashville, Tenn.: Broadman, 1930).

2. Joseph H. Thayer, *Thayers' Greek English Lexicon of the New Testament* (Peabody, MA: Hendrickson, 1889).

3. Harry R. Boer, *A Short History of the Early Church* (Grand Rapids: Eerdmans, 1990), 42.

4. Alexander Roberts and James Donaldson, eds., *Ante-Nicene Fathers: The Writings of the Fathers down to A.D. 325*, Vol. 7 (1886), 320.

5. Rosemary Radford Ruether, *Christianity and Social Systems Historical Constructions and Ethical Challenges* (Lanham: Rowman & Littlefield, 2008), 31.

6. Philip Schaff and Henry Wace, eds., *A Select Library of the Nicene and Post-Nicene Fathers of the Christian Church, Second Series: The Seven Ecumenical Councils*, Vol. 14 (Buffalo: Christian Literature, 1890).

7. James Harvey Robinson, *Readings in European History: A Collection of Extracts from the Sources Chosen with the Purpose of Illustrating the Progress of Culture in Western Europe since the German Invasions*, Vol. 1 (Boston: Ginn & Co., 1905), 66-67.

8. Ruether, *Christianity and Social Systems Historical Constructions and Ethical Challenges*, 13-14.

9. *Ibid.*

10. *Ibid.*

11. Henry Bettenson, ed., *Documents of the Christian Church* (London: Oxford UP, 1943), 31.

12. Johann Peter Kirsch, "Pope St. Leo I (the Great)," *The Catholic Encyclopedia*, Vol. 9 (New York: Robert Appleton, 1910), accessed April 25, 2015, http://www.newadvent.org/cathen/09154b.htm.

13. *Ibid.*

14. Robinson, *Readings in European History*, Vol. 1, 49-50.

15. Bronwen Neil, *Leo the Great* (London: Routledge, 2009), 50.

16. Arthur Barnes, "Saint John Lateran," *The Catholic Encyclopedia*, Vol. 9 (New York: Robert Appleton, 1910), accessed April 26, 2015, http://www. newadvent.org/cathen/09014b.htm.

17. Michael Hines, "Growth of Papal Power," *Teachinghearts*, accessed April 26, 2015, http://www. christianchronicler.com/history1/growth_of_papal_ power.html

18. *Ibid.*

19. *Ibid.*

20. Laverna Patterson, "History of the Empires in Bible Prophecy," accessed April 26, 2015, http://www. teachinghearts.org/dre04histempires.html.

21. Schaff and Wace, eds., *A Select Library of the Nicene and Post-Nicene Fathers of the Christian Church, Second Series: The Seven Ecumenical Councils*, Vol. 6.

22. J. Rickard, "*Clovis I, king of the Franks, r.481-511,*" January 1, 2013, http://www.historyofwar.org/ articles/people_clovis_I.html

23. Robinson, *Readings in European History*, Vol. 1, 52-54.

24. *Ibid.*

25. *Ibid.*

26. *Ibid.*, 35-36.

27. Walter Copland Perry, *The Franks, from Their First Appearance in History to the Death of King Pepin* (Longman, Brown, Green, Longmans, and Roberts, 1857), 88.

28. "History of the Christian Church, Volume IV: Mediaeval Christianity. A.D. 590-1073," *Christian Classics Ethereal Library*, accessed June 23, 2015, http://www.ccel.org/ccel/schaff/hcc4.i.ii.xvii.html.

29. Perry, *Franks*, 85.

30. R. W. Church, *The Beginning of the Middle Ages* (HardPress, 2013), 38-39.

31. Adrian Fortescue, "Justinian I," *The Catholic Encyclopedia*, Vol. 8 (New York: Robert Appleton, 1910), accessed April 26, 2015, http://www.newadvent.org/cathen/08578b.htm.

32. James Allan Evans, "Roman Emperors - DIR Justinian," *De Imperatoribus Romanis, An Online Encyclopedia of Roman Emperors*, accessed April 29, 2015, http://www.roman-emperors.org/justinia.htm.

33. Fortescue, "Justinian I."

34. Patterson, "History of the Empires"

35. "Turning Point Descriptions:" *NYSED Global History and Geography Online Resource Guide*, New York State Education Department, accessed May 11, 2015, http://www.p12.nysed.gov/ciai/socst/ghgonline/turnpoint/textbox_descriptions.html.

36. "Code of Justinian," *Encyclopedia Britannica*, accessed May 11, 2015, http://global.britannica.com/topic/Code-of-Justinian.

37. Talib, "Religious Communications," *The Christian Observer* 9.4 (1810): 193-96.

38. S.P. Scott, *Corpus Juris Civilis* (*The Civil Law, the Code of Justinian*), Vol. 12 (Cincinnati: Central Trust, 1932), 11-12.

39. Georgy Croly, *The Apocalypse of St. John* (E. Littell, 1827), 115.

40. Scott, *Corpus Juris Civilis*, 10-11.

41. Talib, "Religious Communications," 195.

42. Scott, *Corpus Juris Civilis,* 125.
43. Milton V. Anastos, "8. Justinian I and His Relations with Rome," *Myriobiblos Library,* accessed May 11, 2015, http://www.myriobiblos.gr/texts/english/milton1_8.html.
44. *Ibid.*
45. *Encyclopedia Britannica* (Encyclopedia Britannica Ltd., 1941 edition).
46. Dusty Peterson and Elizabeth McDonald, "The Dragnet Behind Alpha, Vineyard, 'Purpose-Driven', 'Toronto' etc," *Bayith Ministries,* accessed April 6, 2016, http://www.users.globalnet.co.uk/~emcd/index32.pdf.
47. *Ibid.,* Used with permission.

CHAPTER 6

1. "List of Famines," *Wikipedia,* accessed September 22, 2011, http://en.wikipedia.org/wiki/List_of_famines.
2. Billie Leff, Navin Ramankutty, and Jonathan A. Foley, "Geographic Distribution of Major Crops across the World," *Global Biogeochem. Cycles* 18.GB1009 (2004).
3. *Ibid.*
4. Joseph H. Thayer, *Thayers' Greek English Lexicon of the New Testament* (Peabody, MA: Hendrickson, 1889).
5. Leff, Ramankutty, and Foley, "Geographic Distribution of Major Crops."
6. Thayer, *Greek English Lexicon of the New Testament.*
7. *Ibid.*
8. *Ibid.*
9. Matthew White, "Selected Death Tolls for Wars, Massacres and Atrocities Before the 20th Century,"

Necrometrics, accessed February 2, 2012, http://necrometrics.com/pre1700a.htm.

10. Paul E. Lovejoy, *Transformations in Slavery: A History of Slavery in Africa* (Cambridge UP, 2000), 26.

11. Adam Hochschild, "Human Cargo: A Study of the Little-known Slave Trade in the Islamic World," *New York Times on the Web*, March 4, 2001, accessed May 1, 2015, https://www.nytimes.com/books/01/03/04/reviews/010304.04hochsct.html.

12. Leff, Ramankutty, and Foley, "Geographic Distribution of Major Crops."

13. Jill Dubisch, "Cyclades," *Encyclopedia.com* (HighBeam Research, 1996), accessed May 1, 2015, http://www.encyclopedia.com/topic/Cyclades.aspx.

14. Eric Rymer, "Farming in Ancient Greece," *Farming in Ancient Greece*, History Source LLC, accessed May 1, 2015, http://historylink101.com/2/greece3/jobs-farming.htm.

15. Thayer, *Greek English Lexicon of the New Testament*.

16. *Ibid.*

17. Robert Jamieson, A. R. Fausset, and David Brown, *A Commentary on the Old and New Testaments* (1871).

18. Albert Barnes, *Albert Barnes' Notes on the Bible* (Grand Rapids: Baker, 1885).

19. David E. Aune, *Revelation 6-16: Word Biblical Commentary*, Vol. 52B (Nashville: Thomas Nelson, 1998).

20. Paul Halsall, "Famine of 1315," *Fordham University: The Jesuit University of New York* (Internet Medieval Source Book, 1996), accessed April 19, 2012, http://legacy.fordham.edu/halsall/source/famin1315a.asp.

21. "European Feudalism," *European Feudalism,* Siteseen Ltd., accessed May 18, 2013, http://www.lordsandladies.org/european-feudalism.htm.

22. Henri Pirenne, *Medieval Cities: Their Origins and the Revival of Trade: (2. Printing)* (Princeton, NJ: Princeton UP, 1944), 26.

23. *Ibid.*

24. Credit: Tariq ibn Ziyad, https://commons.wikimedia.org/wiki/File:Map_of_expansion_of_Caliphate.svg.

25. "Serfdom," *Encyclopaedia Britannica,* accessed May 22, 2016, http://www.britannica.com/topic/serfdom.

26. *Ibid.*

27. "State and Society in the High Middle Ages (1000-1300)," accessed May 22, 2016, http://facstaff.bloomu.edu/hickey/state_and_society_in_the_high_mi.htm.

28. Marc Bloch, *Feudal Society, Volume I: The Growth of Ties of Dependence* (Routledge & Kegan Paul Ltd., 1962).

29. E.P. Cheyney, "Oath to a Lord -- from the 9th Century," *Trans., University of Pennsylvania Translations and Reprints* IV.3 (1898) (University of Pennsylvania Press), accessed May 3, 2015, http://www.calvin.edu/academic/medieval/village/feud1.htm.

30. Bloch, *Feudal Society, Volume I.*

31. "State and Society in the High Middle Ages (1000-1300)," accessed May 22, 2016, http://facstaff.bloomu.edu/hickey/state_and_society_in_the_high_mi.htm.

32. "Peasant Life in the Middle Ages," *Camelot International: Britain's Heritage and History*, accessed May 24, 2016, http://www.camelotintl.com/village/peasant.html.

33. *Ibid.*

34. "The Domesday Book Online," *The Domesday Book Online – Home*, accessed May 18, 2013, http://www.domesdaybook.co.uk.

35. J. P. Sommerville, "Medieval English Society," *Medieval English Society*, University of Wisconsin–Madison, accessed May 18, 2013, http://faculty.history.wisc.edu/sommerville/123/123 13 Society.htm.

36. "Life of Peasantry (Serfs) in the Middle Ages," *Medieval Times RSS2*, accessed May 18, 2013, http://www.medievaltimes.info/medieval-life-and-society/life-of-peasantry-serfs-in-the-middle-ages.

37. Sommerville, "Medieval English Society."

38. *Ibid.*

39. *Ibid.*

40. *Ibid.*

41. Steven Kreis, "Lecture 22 European Agrarian Society: Manorialism," *History Guide, Lectures on Ancient and Medieval Europe History*, accessed May 18, 2013, http://historyguide.org/ancient/lecture22b.html.

42. *Ibid.*

43. Chris Trueman, "The Lifestyle of Medieval Peasants," *The History Learning Site*, accessed May 18, 2013, http://www.historylearningsite.co.uk/medieval_peasants.htm.

44. "Medieval Food & Cooking," *Life In A Medieval Castle: Medieval Food*, C&MH, accessed May 18,

2013, http://www.castlesandmanorhouses.com/ life_04_food.htm.

45. *Ibid.*
46. *Ibid.*
47. *Ibid.*
48. *Ibid.*
49. "Life of Peasantry (Serfs) in the Middle Ages," *Medieval Times RSS2*, accessed May 18, 2013, http:// www.medievaltimes.info/medieval-life-and-society/ life-of-peasantry-serfs-in-the-middle-ages.
50. Karl Marx and Ben Fowkes, *Capital: A Critique of Political Economy*, Vol. 1 (England: Penguin, 1976), 875.

CHAPTER 7

1. "Selected Death Tolls for Wars, Massacres and Atrocities Before the 20th Century," *Users.erols.com,* accessed January 24, 2011.
2. C. P. Fitzgerald, *China: A Short Cultural History* (Westview, 1985), 314.
3. Joseph H. Thayer, *Thayers' Greek English Lexicon of the New Testament* (Peabody, MA: Hendrickson, 1889).
4. *Ibid.*
5. *Ibid.*
6. *Ibid.*
7. *Ibid.*
8. *Ibid.*
9. *Ibid.*
10. *Ibid.*
11. *Ibid.*
12. *Ibid.*

13. Jonathan Porter Berkey, *The Formation of Islam: Religion and Society in the Near East, 600-1800* (New York: Cambridge UP, 2003), 72.
14. *Ibid.*
15. Moše Šārôn, *Studies in Islamic History and Civilization: In Honour of Professor David Ayalon* (Jerusalem: Cana, 1986), 108.
16. *Ibid.*, 109.
17. Kelly Phillips Erb, "Islamic State Warns Christians: Convert, Pay Tax, Leave or Die," *Forbes,* July 19, 2014, accessed May 5, 2015, http://www.forbes.com/sites#/sites/kellyphillipserb/2014/07/19/islamic-state-warns-christians-convert-pay-tax-leave-or-die/#6cd2218e3718.
18. Thomas Patrick Hughes, *A Dictionary of Islam Being a Cyclopaedia of the Doctrines, Rites, Ceremonies, and Customs, Together with the Technical and Theological Terms, of the Muhammadan Religion* (London: W.H. Allen & Company, 1895), 129.
19. Diane Morgan, *Essential Islam: A Comprehensive Guide to Belief and Practice* (Santa Barbara, Calif.: ABC-CLIO, 2010), 87.
20. Hughes, *Dictionary of Islam,* 243.
21. Morgan, *Essential Islam,* 87-88.
22. *Ibid.*
23. *Ibid.*
24. *Ibid.*, 88-89.
25. *Ibid.*, 92.
26. *Ibid.*
27. *Ibid.*
28. *Ibid.*

29. *Ibid.*
30. Berkey, *The Formation of Islam: Religion and Society in the Near East, 600-1800,* 72-73.
31. *Ibid..*
32. *Ibid.*
33. Majid Khadduri, *The Islamic Law of Nations: Shaybānī's Siyar* (Baltimore: Johns Hopkins, 1966), 38-39.
34. C. G. Weeramantry, *Justice without Frontiers: Furthering Human Rights, Vol. 1* (The Hague: Kluwer Law International, 1997), 136.
35. *Ibid.*
36. Khadduri, *The Islamic Law of Nations,* 57-59.
37. *Ibid.*
38. *Ibid.*
39. *Ibid.*
40. Wael B. Hallaq, "Was Al-Shafii the Master Architect of Islamic Jurisprudence?" *Int. J. Middle East Stud.* 25.4 (1993): 587-605.
41. *Ibid.*
42. Khadduri, *The Islamic Law of Nations,* 8.
43. *Ibid.*
44. Erb, "Islamic State Warns Christians: Convert, Pay Tax, Leave or Die."

CHAPTER 8

1. "European Wars of Religion," *Wikipedia*, accessed February 2, 2012, http://en.wikipedia.org/wiki/European_wars_of_religion.
2. "List of Wars by Death Toll," *Wikipedia*, accessed February 2, 2012, http://en.wikipedia.org/wiki/List_of_wars_by_death_toll.

3.   Matthew White, "Selected Death Tolls for Wars, Massacres and Atrocities Before the 20th Century," *Necrometrics*, accessed February 2, 2012, http://necrometrics.com/pre1700a.htm.

4.   "Eighty Years' War," *FindTheData*, Graphiq, Inc., accessed June 7, 2016, http://wars.findthedata.com/l/135/Eighty-Years-War.

5.   M. J. Spalding, *The History of the Protestant Reformation: In Germany and Switzerland : And in England, Ireland, Scotland, the Netherlands, France, and Northern Europe : In a Series of Essays, Reviewing D'Aubigné, Menzel, Hallan, Bishop Short, Prescott, Ranké, Fryxell,* 2nd ed. (Louisville, KY.: Webb & Levering, 1861).

6.   Gerald Strauss, ed., *Manifestations of Discontent in Germany on the Eve of the Reformation: A Collection of Documents* (Bloomington: Indiana UP, 1971).

7.   Pérez Zagorín, *Rebels and Rulers, 1500–1660* (Cambridge UP, 1984).

8.   Helmut Meyer, "Kappel, Guerre Di," accessed February 2, 2012, http://hls-dhs-dss.ch/textes/i/I8903.php.

9.   "Image: Germany. The Schmalkaldic War (1547-1554)," *CosmoLearning*, accessed February 2, 2012, https://cosmolearning.org/images/germany-the-schmalkaldic-war-1547-1554/.

10. "The 80 Years War and the Spanish Armada," *Study.com*, accessed May 26, 2016, http://study.com/academy/lesson/the-80-years-war-and-the-spanish-armada.html.

11. Mack P. Holt, *The French Wars of Religion, 1562–1629,* 2nd Edition (Cambridge University Press, 2005).

12. Ian Gentles, citing John Morrill's reminder, states, "there is no stable, agreed title for the events…. They have been variously labeled the Great Rebellion, the Puritan Revolution, the English Civil War, the English Revolution, and most recently, the Wars of the Three Kingdoms." See I. J. Gentles, *The English Revolution and the Wars in the Three Kingdoms, 1638-1652* (Harlow, England: Pearson/Longman, 2007), 3.

13. "Thirty Years' War," *History.com*, accessed May 26, 2016, http://www.history.com/topics/thirty-years-war.

14. Geoffrey Parker, ed., *The Thirty Years' War*, 2nd ed. (London: Routledge, 1997), 139.

15. "The Thirty Years' War," *Czech Republic - The Official Website*, Ministry of Foreign Affairs of the Czech Republic, accessed February 16, 2012, http://www.czech.cz/en/czech-republic/history/all-about-czech-history/the-thirty-years-war/.

16. C. James Johnston Jr, "Coins of the Thirty Years War," *The Wonderful World of Coins* (Journal of Antiques & Collectibles, 2004), accessed February 14, 2015, http://www.journalofantiques.com/Jan04/coinsjan04.htm.

17. Samuel Rawson Gardiner, *The Thirty Years' War, 1618-1648* (New York: C. Scribner's Sons., 1887).

18. Bamber Gascoigne, History of "Cuius Regio, Eius Religio," *Historyworld*, From 2001, ongoing, accessed February 16, 2012, http://www.historyworld.net/wrldhis/PlainTextHistories.asp?ParagraphID=how.

19. *Ibid.*

20. Parker, ed., *The Thirty Years' War*, 2nd ed., 17.

21. Hajo Holborn, *A History of Modern Germany* (Princeton UP, 1982).

22. "Peace of Westphalia," *Oxford Bibliographies*, accessed July 16, 2015, http://www.oxfordbibliographies. com/view/document/obo-9780199743292/obo-9780199743292-0073.xml.

23. "Martyrs Mirror Images," *Mennonite Library and Archives* (Bethel College), accessed February 16, 2012, http://www.bethelks.edu/mla/holdings/scans/ martyrsmirror/.

24. Thieleman J. Van Braght, and I. Daniel Rupp, *The Bloody Theatre, or Martyrs' Mirror, of the Defenceless Christians: Who Suffered and Were Put to Death for the Testimony of Jesus, Their Savior, from the Time of Christ until the Year A.D. 1660* (Near Lampeter Square, Lancaster Co., Pa.: David Miller, 1837).

25. Rich Preheim, "Atonement for 2 Centuries of Persecution; Catholic, Protestant Churches Repent of Efforts to Eliminate Anabaptists," *The Washington Post,* June 19, 2004, accessed February 9, 2012, http://www.highbeam.com/doc/1P2-185506. html.

CHAPTER 9

1. "Historic World Earthquakes," *Earthquake Hazards Program, United States Geological Survey,* accessed September 28, 2011, http://earthquake.usgs.gov/ earthquakes/world/historical.php.

2. "Historic World Earthquakes," *Earthquake Hazards Program.*

3. L. A. Mendes-Victor, C. Sousa Oliveira, J. Azevedo, and A. Ribeiro, eds., *The 1755 Lisbon Earthquake Revisited* (Dordrecht: Springer, 2009), 43.
4. *Ibid.*, 7.
5. *Ibid.*, 45-46.
6. M.-A. Gutscher, M.A. Baptista, and J.M. Miranda, "The Gibraltar Arc Seismogenic Zone (part 2): Constraints on a Shallow East Dipping Fault Plane Source for the 1755 Lisbon Earthquake Provided by Tsunami Modeling and Seismic Intensity," *Tectonophysics* 426 (2006): 153-66 (Elsevier B.V.), accessed March 20, 2011, http://www.sciencedirect. com/science/article/pii/S0040195106002897.
7. Alvaro S. Pereira, "The Opportunity of a Disaster: The Economic Impact of the 1755 Lisbon Earthquake," *J. Eco. History* 69.2009.2 (2009): 466-99.
8. Mendes-Victor, *1755 Lisbon Earthquake*, 44.
9. *Ibid.*, 46.
10. *Ibid.*, 44.
11. *Ibid.*, 49.
12. *Ibid.*, 47.
13. *Ibid.*
14. *Ibid.*
15. *Ibid.*
16. *Ibid.*
17. T. D. Kendrick, *The Lisbon Earthquake* (Philadelphia: J. B. Lippincott, 1955).
18. Mendes-Victor, *1755 Lisbon Earthquake*, 8-9.
19. *Ibid.*, 9.
20. *Ibid.*
21. *Ibid.*

22. *Ibid.*, 51.
23. *Ibid.*, 50-51.

CHAPTER 10

1. Mark Strauss, "Ten Notable Apocalypses That (Obviously) Didn't Happen," *Smithsonian Magazine*, November 12, 2009, accessed September 9, 2011, http://www.smithsonianmag.com/history/ten-notable-apocalypses-that-obviously-didnt-happen-9126331/?no-ist=.

2. Keith C. Heidorn, "New England's Dark Day," *Weather Almanac for May 2004*, The Weather Doctor's Weather Almanac, accessed February 16, 2012, http://www.islandnet.com/~see/weather/almanac/arc2004/alm04may.htm.

3. *Ibid.*

4. Samuel Williams, "An Account of a very uncommon Dark Days, in the State of New England, May 19, 1780," in *The Analytical Review, or History of Literature, Domestic and Foreign, on an Enlarged Plan*, Vol. 2 (London: Printed for J. Johnson [etc.], 1788), 519.

5. Samuel Tenney, (December 1785), "Dr. Tenney's Letter on the Dark Day, May 19, 1780," in *Collections of the Massachusetts Historical Society, For the Year 1792*, Vol. 1 (Boston: Re-printed by Munroe & Francis, Court-Street, 1806), 95-98.

6. T. J. Campanella, "'Mark Well the Gloom': Shedding Light on the Great Dark Day of 1780," *Environmental History* 12 (2007): 35-58.

7. *Ibid.*

8. *Ibid.*
9. Experience Wight Richardson and Ellen R. Glueck, *Diary of Experience (Wight) Richardson, Sudbury, Mass. 1728-1782* (Boston: Massachusetts Historical Society, 1978).
10. *Samuel Phillips Savage Diaries, 1770-1795* (Boston: Massachusetts Historical Society).
11. *Massachusetts Spy,* May 25, 1780.
12. Campanella, "Mark Well the Gloom."
13. *Ibid.*
14. *Ibid.*
15. John Greenleaf Whittier, "Abraham Davenport," *The Complete Poetical Works of John Greenleaf Whittier,* Household ed. (Boston: Houghton, Osgood and Company, 1880), 312-313.
16. Campanella, "Mark Well the Gloom."
17. *Ibid.*
18. *Ibid.*
19. *Ibid.*
20. *Ibid.*
21. *Ibid.*
22. *Ibid.*
23. *Ibid.*
24. *Ibid.*
25. *Ibid.*
26. Viator, *Independent Chronicle,* May 25, 1780.
27. Campanella, "Mark Well the Gloom."
28. *Ibid*
29. *Ibid.*
30. *Ibid.*
31. "Eclipse Predictions by Fred Espenak (NASA's GSFC)," *Five Millennium Catalog of Solar Eclipses:*

1701 to 1800, accessed October 6, 2011, http://eclipse.gsfc.nasa.gov/SEcat5/SE1701-1800.html.

32. Campanella, "Mark Well the Gloom."

33. *Ibid.*

34. *Independent Chronicle*, June 15, 1780, Published as *The Independent Chronicle and the Universal Advertiser*, 12.616 (Boston, MA).

35. Campanella, "Mark Well the Gloom."

36. *Ibid.*

37. *Ibid.*

38. *Ibid.*

39. Dave Thurlow, "Revolutionary Warm Spell," *The Weather Notebook*, accessed October 6, 2011, http://www.weathernotebook.org/transcripts/1999/04/07.html.

40. *Samuel Phillips Savage Diaries, 1770-1795.*

41. Campanella, "Mark Well the Gloom."

42. Matthew Dingley, "Glossary: A's," *NWS JetStream*, National Oceanic and Atmospheric Administration, accessed October 7, 2011, http://www.srh.noaa.gov/jetstream/append/glossary_a.htm.

43. Viator, *Independent Chronicle.*

44. Letter from "A Well Wisher to *Science*," to "Messrs. Printers," *Independent Ledger*, June 5, 1780.

45. "Eclipse Predictions by Fred Espenak (NASA's GSFC)," *Five Millennium Catalog of Lunar Eclipses: 1701 to 1800*, National Aeronautics and Space Administration, accessed October 6, 2011, http://eclipse.gsfc.nasa.gov/LEcat5/LE1701-1800.html.

46. "Visual Appearance of Lunar Eclipses," *Five Millennium Canon of Lunar Eclipses [Espenak and Meeus]*, National Aeronautics and Space

Administration, accessed October 7, 2011, http://eclipse.gsfc.nasa.gov/LEcat5/appearance.html.

CHAPTER 11

1. Denison Olmsted, "ART. XIV.--Observations on the Meteors of November 13th, 1833," *The American Journal of Science and Arts* 25.2: 363-411, (Biodiversity Heritage Library), accessed May 8, 2015, http://www.biodiversitylibrary.org/page/30964366#page/383/mode/1up.
2. *Ibid.*
3. "Nov 12, 1799: First Meteor Shower on Record," *This Day in History*, A&E Television Networks, accessed October 11, 2011, http://www.history.com/this-day-in-history/first-meteor-shower-on-record.
4. "Brief History of the Leonid Shower," *Leonid MAC*, National Aeronautics and Space Administration, accessed October 11, 2011, http://leonid.arc.nasa.gov/history.html.
5. *Ibid.*
6. Olmsted, "Meteors of November 13th, 1833."
7. *Ibid.*
8. *Ibid.*
9. *Ibid.*
10. *Ibid.*
11. *Ibid.*
12. *Ibid.*
13. *Ibid.*
14. *Ibid.*
15. *Ibid.*
16. *Ibid.*
17. *Ibid.*

18. *Ibid.*
19. *Ibid.*
20. Woodcut print image of the Leonids on November 13, 1833. According to *Mechanics' Magazine*, this illustration was made by Mr. Pickering, who "witnessed the scene" at Niagara Falls, New York, accessed October 11, 2011, http://en.wikipedia.org/wiki/File:Leonids-Pickering.jpg.
21. Olmsted, "Meteors of November 13th, 1833."
22. James Strong, *Strong's Hebrew and Greek Dictionaries* (1890).
23. Olmsted, "Meteors of November 13th, 1833."
24. *Ibid.*
25. *Ibid.*

CHAPTER 12

1. Judith Zachariasen, Kerry Sieh, Frederick W. Taylor, R. Lawrence Edwards, and Wahyoe S. Hantoro. "Submergence and Uplift Associated with the Giant 1833 Sumatran Subduction Earthquake: Evidence from Coral Microatolls." *J. Geophys. Res.* 104.B1 (1999): 895-919. *California Institute of Technology Tectonics Observatory*. Web. 19 Oct. 2011. http://www.tectonics.caltech.edu/sumatra/downloads/papers/P99a.pdf.
2. "Glossary - Subduction," *Volcano Hazards Program*, U.S. Geological Survey, accessed June 4, 2016, http://volcanoes.usgs.gov/vsc/glossary/subduction.html.
3. "Giant Megathrust Earthquakes," *Natural Resources Canada*, Service Canada, accessed October 15,

2011, http://earthquakescanada.nrcan.gc.ca/zones/ cascadia/mega-eng.php.

4. *Ibid.*

5. Phil Cummins and Mark Leonard, "The Boxing Day 2004 Tsunami—A Repeat of the 1833 Tsunami?" *Geoscience Australia* 77 (2005), *AusGeo News March 2005 Issue No. 77*, Geoscience Australia, accessed October 19, 2011, http://www.ga.gov.au/ ausgeonews/ausgeonews200503/tsunami.jsp.

6. "Such massive earthquakes only occur in subduction zones where two of the rigid tectonic plates that comprise the earth's surface are converging, and one plate, usually composed of heavier oceanic material, dives beneath another, usually composed of lighter continental material." (*Ibid.*)

7. "Magnitude 9.0 - NEAR THE EAST COAST OF HONSHU, JAPAN," *Earthquake Hazards Program*, U.S. Geological Survey, accessed June 20, 2015, http://earthquake.usgs.gov/earthquakes/ eqinthenews/2011/usc0001xgp/#summary.

8. "Magnitude 8.8 - OFFSHORE BIO-BIO, CHILE," *Earthquake Hazards Program*, U.S. Geological Survey, accessed October 19, 2011, http://earthquake. usgs.gov/earthquakes/eqinthenews/2010/ us2010tfan/#summary.

9. Danny Hilman Natawidjaja, Kerry Sieh, Mohamed Chlieh, John Galetzka, Bambang W. Suwargadi, Hai Cheng, R. Lawrence Edwards, Jean-Philippe Avouac, and Steven N. Ward, "Source Parameters of the Great Sumatran Megathrust Earthquakes of 1797 and 1833 Inferred from Coral Microatolls,"

J. Geophys. Res. 111.B6 (2006), *Journal of Geophysical Research*, AGU Publications, accessed October 24, 2011, http://onlinelibrary.wiley.com/doi/10.1029/2005JB004025/full.

10. Kerry Sieh and Danny Natawidjaja, "Neotectonics of the Sumatran Fault, Indonesia," *J. Geophys. Res.* 105.B12 (2000): 28295-8326, *California Institute of Technology Tectonics Observatory*, accessed October 24, 2011, http://www.tectonics.caltech.edu/sumatra/downloads/papers/P00e.pdf.

11. Natawidjaja et al., "Great Sumatran Megathrust Earthquakes."

12. *Ibid.*

13. Francie Diep, "Fast Facts about the Japan Earthquake and Tsunami," *Scientific American Global RSS*, Scientific American, March 14, 2011, accessed October 19, 2011, http://www.scientificamerican.com/article/fast-facts-japan.

14. Natawidjaja et al., "Great Sumatran Megathrust Earthquakes."

15. *Ibid.*

16. José C. Borrero, Kerry Sieh, Mohamed Chlieh, and Costas E. Synolakis, "Tsunami Inundation Modeling for Western Sumatra," *Proceedings of the National Academy of Sciences of USA* 103.52 (2006): 19673-19677, accessed October 19, 2011, http://www.pnas.org/content/103/52/19673.full.

17. Zachariasen et al., "Submergence and Uplift Associated with the Giant 1833 Sumatran Subduction Earthquake."

18. *Ibid.*

19. *Ibid.*

20. *Ibid.*
21. Natawidjaja et al., "Great Sumatran Megathrust Earthquakes."
22. Photo courtesy of the U.S. Geological Survey.
23. Natawidjaja et al., "Great Sumatran Megathrust Earthquakes."
24. *Ibid.*
25. Alan Buis, "Chilean Quake May Have Shortened Earth Days," *News*, National Aeronautics and Space Administration, March 1, 2010, accessed October 21, 2011, http://www.nasa.gov/topics/earth/features/earth-20100301.html.
26. *Ibid.*
27. "Japan Quake Is 5th Largest in World since 1900," *CBS News*, March 11, 2011, CBS News, accessed October 21, 2011, http://www.cbsnews.com/news/japan-quake-is-5th-largest-in-world-since-1900.
28. Evans Vanessa, "Earth's Day Length Shortened by Japan Earthquake," *ConvenienTruth*, March 14, 2011, accessed October 27, 2011, https://convenietruth.wordpress.com/2011/03/14/scientists-say-earthquake-caused-shift-in-earths-axis/.
29. Richard Gross, "Japan Earthquake May Have Shifted Earth's Axis," *NPR*, March 18, 2011, accessed October 27, 2011, http://www.npr.org/2011/03/18/134658880/Japan-Earthquake-May-Have-Changed-Earths-Axis.
30. *Ibid.*
31. T. J. Campanella, "'Mark Well the Gloom': Shedding Light on the Great Dark Day of 1780," *Environmental History* 12 (2007): 35-58.

32. L. A. Mendes-Victor, C. Sousa Oliveira, J. Azevedo, and A. Ribeiro, eds., *The 1755 Lisbon Earthquake Revisited* (Dordrecht: Springer, 2009).

CHAPTER 13

1. Surendre M. Verma, *The Mystery of the Tunguska Fireball* (Cambridge: Totem, 2006).
2. *Ibid.*
3. John Engledew, *The Tungus Event or The Great Siberian Meteorite* (New York: Algora Pub., 2010).
4. Alexander Bagrov, "Tunguska Meteorite: A Warning from Outer Space," *Sputnik News*, Trend News Agency, March 6, 2008, accessed November 28, 2011, http://sputniknews.com/analysis/20080306/100847639.html#ixzz48yKYLrVL.
5. *Ibid.*
6. Verma, *The Mystery of the Tunguska Fireball.*
7. *Ibid.*
8. Bagrov, "Tunguska Meteorite: A Warning from Outer Space."
9. Verma, *The Mystery of the Tunguska Fireball.*
10. *Ibid.*
11. *Ibid.*
12. *Ibid.*
13. *Ibid.*
14. *Ibid.*
15. *Ibid.*
16. *Ibid.*
17. *Ibid.*
18. *Ibid.*
19. James Strong, *Strong's Hebrew and Greek Dictionaries* (1890).

20. Joseph H. Thayer, *Thayers' Greek English Lexicon of the New Testament* (Peabody, MA: Hendrickson, 1889).
21. Strong, *Strong's Hebrew and Greek Dictionaries.*
22. Verma, *The Mystery of the Tunguska Fireball.*
23. Chris Trayner, "The Tunguska event," *Journal of the British Astronomical Association* 107 (1997): 117-130.
24. Engledew, *The Tungus Event or The Great Siberian Meteorite.*
25. Thayer, *Greek English Lexicon of the New Testament.*